Putting FUN Back Into
FUNdraising!

Putting FUN Back Into
FUNdraising!

Raise more money in one night than
five years of bake sales, car washes or
pancake breakfasts

by Cal and Jeanne Gormick

Copyright

Putting FUN Back Into FUNdraising
by Cal and Jeanne Gormick

Copyright © 2012, 2019 by Cal and Jeanne Gormick

ISBN: 978-0-9623816-9-0

Library of Congress Control Number: 2012933269

Published by Gormick's All American
Laguna Niguel, CA 92677

Printed in the United States of America.

Cover design by Lisa Hainline
www.lionsgatebookdesign.com

Interior layout by Edie Glaser
www.craftingstones.com

To all the truly dedicated nonprofit volunteers, who have permitted Gormick's All American FUNdraising Team to help them reach their FUNdraising goals; we dedicate this book. We believe it will bring a new experience of enthusiasm and creativity to a difficult task.

A special thanks to the Niguel Parent Participation Preschool, which launched us on our very exciting career and to our entire family and our many friends for their patience and affectionate support.

Minor Disclaimer

The authors have attempted to cover all areas of concern that relate to producing a FUNd-raising Goods and Services Auction based upon their own personal experience. However, since laws and regulations vary from state to state and the authors are not tax consultants, agents of the state, or insurance experts, it is the responsibility of each organization to check all restrictions and regulations prior to holding any FUNdraising event.

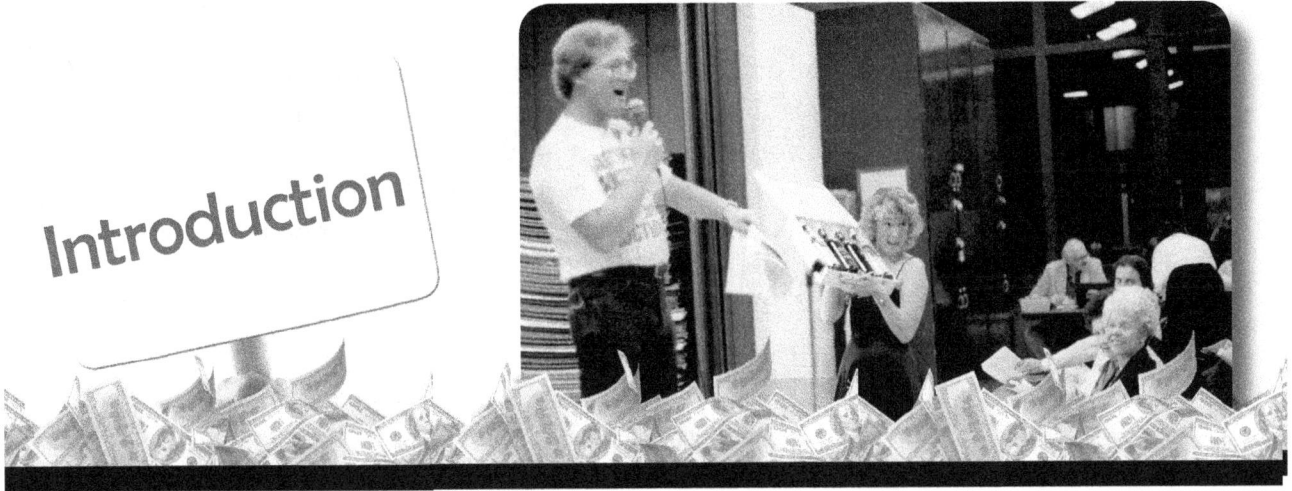

Introduction

Two words that describe a successful FUNdraising event are "BE ORGANIZED." Raising funds is just like running a profitable business. If things are well planned and directed, you will receive a great deal of support. If you run a chaotic, disorganized fundraising effort your volunteers will lose interest and commitment. Once that occurs, your membership will not be as supportive and the success of your fundraiser will be in jeopardy.

Knowing these things, Cal and I were determined to design a syllabus with the proper step-by-step guidelines for use by literally every nonprofit organization. We have taken our own personal experiences and described methods we have actually used successfully. Now we have updated and created an effective tool for the 21st century.

"FUNdraising can be FUN!" Goods and Services Auctions can provide substantially large profits for your organization. They are unique, because they pull people together to share in the excitement of a BIG SOCIAL EVENT with some REAL BARGAINS!

We have a philosophy, which differs from many fundraising auction experts. Rather than being set-up as an elegant affair for the wealthy, we have created a successful FUNdraising event designed for the masses.

Every Committee we have worked with has asked the same initial questions: "Will the event be a success? How much money can we raise? Where do we start to get Donations? How do we get Donations?" This is why we wrote down our success formula in the first place and why we worked very closely with all of our clients. Part of our joy was being able to see them receive the justly deserved praise for all their hard work. We believe our techniques will help millions more volunteers all around the world.

In addition to the fellowship that takes place with our Auctions when the volunteers meet each other on new levels, a real team spirit is developed. This is so necessary when trying to achieve new financial goals. Other members and friends also enjoy coming to these Auctions not only because of the exciting bargains they can expect to purchase, but because these events are well attended social mixers.

We recommend that organizations schedule their Auctions early in their calendar year, so that they can have a clearer picture of the money they have to work with to meet their budget deadlines. This makes their programs more efficient.

NOTE: A company or group of individuals can also use our formula to raise funds for any non-profit cause. A less formal structure works quite well. Often many thousands of dollars are raised at a company-sponsored party designed to entertain clients, suppliers, sub-contractors, employees, etc. This can be VERY EFFECTIVE in creating a good community image for the company, especially if proper Publicity is done after the event.

Jeanne and Cal

Table of Contents

1

Backdating & Overall Plan

If you already have a team in place and have prior fundraising experience, you may only need this chapter to run a very successful Event! We recommend, however, that you read through this entire book to obtain the best perspective on the project.

Copies of forms referred to within this manual can be found in the back of this book.

One really important key to success: The entire Committee should believe from day one that this Event is to be the biggest, best and most entertaining FUNdraising Event of the Year!

On the next few pages is a Backdating Calendar list of things and completion deadlines. Please note that a Google Calendar or similar can be created for access by your Volunteers. The actual dates can be included and made available on-line.

Lines for recording important dates and notes are provided as well as boxes to check off.

3 – 4 Months Before Auction

☐ **1. Set Your Goal** _____

_____

_____

☐ Examine your long and short range goals for FUNdraising.

☐ Determine what this FUNdraiser should net for you. (Just try your best, these numbers can change as time goes by.)

☐ **2. Create Your Budget** - Make a detailed budget to include the following: (Note that MUCH can be donated to cut costs.) _____

_____

_____

☐ First, determine how much money has been allocated from the general budget for your FUNdraising campaign. This indicates how much you have to work with. (You may have to start with nothing!)

☐ **Beverages** - wine and/or beer, mixed drinks, and non-alcoholic punch/soda.

☐ **Food** - may be donated (desserts, hors d'oeuvres, potluck, etc.) KEEP IT SIMPLE to focus on the Auction.

☐ **Tickets** - may be donated by printer or other business.

☐ **Invitations** – Cost of printing can be underwritten by a business. Can be fancy or simple Announcement Flyers.

☐ **Paper Products** - cups, stirrers, plates, napkins, etc. May be donated as business promotional items with company logos or advertising on them.

☐ **Coffee, Creamer, and Sugar** - may be donated by a local Starbucks or other coffee shop.

☐ **Decorations** - flowers may be donated by florist.

☐ **Tablecloths** may also be donated. Dollar stores are a great and inexpensive option.

3 - 4 Months Before Auction

☐ **Stationery Products** - Certificates, envelopes, artwork needs, Publicity Display Posters, Donor Ribbons, pens/pencils (for Silent Auction), etc.

☐ **Three Seasonal Hats** for successful Bidders.

☐ **Receipt Books** - at least 2 copies. One for buyer and one for organization's records.

☐ **Security Guard** - if required by your facility. Also good if you have very valuable, easily stolen items, alcohol is being served, or you expect a large amount of cash at the Auction.

☐ **Postage** - for publicity, donation requests, thank-you letters and invitations.

☐ **Auction Booklet Copies** - a printer may give you a break in exchange for advertising. A business may let you use their copier in exchange for promotion of their company.

☐ **Room Rental** - SECURE THIS LOCATION EARLY!

☐ Ticket prices should be only enough to cover your evening's estimated expenses (from items listed above.) Your profit should come from the Auction itself. Excessive admission prices will turn people away. GET AS MANY PEOPLE THERE AS POSSIBLE! This Event is for the masses!

☐ **3. Select Your Date** _____

☐ Spring and Fall are best (set rain/snow date, if needed in your area.)

☐ Check with Community or Chambers of Commerce Master Calendar and others, if available, to avoid possible date conflicts.

☐ Saturday nights are best; Friday nights next best. Weeknights can be good, when an all day activity such as a golf tournament is combined with the Auction.

☐ Avoid holidays, but design Themes around them.

☐ **4. Secure Your Auction Location NOW!!!** _____

_____

3 – 4 Months Before Auction

☐   Select a site with an open area and/or stage where the entire audience can easily see the Master of Ceremony/Auctioneer. Try to find the most exciting location your budget permits. (We've used airplane hangars, university campuses, country clubs, large estates, etc. Some were even donated!)

☐   **5.**   **Have your Food Chairman watch for good beverage prices**
(possibly get a Donation or a corporate Donor to underwrite the cost.)

_____

☐   **6.**   **Have your Publicity Chairman check on all Publicity requirements** for publications and radio/TV stations. _____

_____

☐   **7.**   **Begin searching for your Master of Ceremony/Auctioneer**
looking for "entertainer-type" personality (NOTE: This is not necessarily a professional auctioneer!)

Notes

_____

_____

_____

_____

_____

_____

_____

_____

_____

Complete As They Come In

8.   Have Donation Chairman send Letters to verify Donations committed, but not yet acquired.

❏   Request that a Certificate or actual Donation be in the hands of your Donation Committee as soon as possible to start preparations for the Auction. Set a final date by which ALL Donations must be in to the Donation Committee.

❏   Be sure your Donation Chairman keeps a carefully organized list of all Donations as they come in. Only those items actually in your Committee's hands should be listed. When a Thank-you Letter is sent to the Donors of these listed items, this should also be checked off this list.

❏   A separate list of promised items can help with follow-up on them.

Complete Monthly Until Auction

9.   Have Publicity Chairman contact the membership
and include in Newsletters, emails and texts the following:

❏   Indicate upcoming Auction every month.

❏   Emphasize need for more Donations and list those that are already in.

❏   Encourage large Ticket Sales and suggest that members hold a pre-Auction private party. If an Incentive is being offered to the member who brings the most people, also mention that.

❏   Continue to emphasize Ticket Sales and list additional Donations that have come in.

❏   Mention pre-Auction party idea again.

_____

_____

2 Months Before Auction

☐ 10. **Hold regular, monthly progress meetings** with your membership, as well as, your key Chairmen. Keep meetings timely, short, positive, and UPBEAT. At your first meeting explain to your membership about the Auction and your NEED FOR CHAIRMEN to make it a successful Event. Begin recruiting Volunteers.

_____

_____

☐ 11. **Have your Telephone/Email Committee contact members individually for donations and volunteer help.**

    ☐ Advertise the upcoming Auction - make a personal appeal.

    ☐ Emphasize an evening filled with excitement, fun, and bargains.

_____

_____

☐ 12. **Instruct your Volunteer Chairmen**

_____

_____

☐ 13. **Have your Donation Chairman train your members** on how to get Donations and present Donation suggestions to all of them. (A list of items to put onto training chart can be found at the back of this book.)

_____

_____

2 Months Before Auction

☐ **14. Send out membership Donation Request Letters**

    ☐ Make this a really "up-tempo" letter.

    ☐ Include the need for Volunteers and emphasize the importance of an EARLY response.

☐ **15. You should now have an idea of membership support levels.**

    ☐ Check merchant support on previous FUNdraising campaigns (door prizes, etc.)

    ☐ Have your Donation Chairman and their Committee approach these Donors and others in your area.

☐ **16. Prepare Request and Thank-You Letters for Donors (members as well as merchants.)**

    ☐ These may be needed for tax purposes and it is the courteous way to help insure Donations for next year.

    ☐ We recommend that these be mailed out as Donations are received. After the Auction, you and your Committee will just want to relax. You may also want to enclose the complimentary Tickets for Donors in these Letters, so they must be sent early.

    ☐ Some merchants may request a Letter prior to your picking up Donations, so have some Letters prepared for your Donation Committee to carry along with their Auction Item Description Sheets. (Samples found in the back of this book.)

---

2 Months Before Auction

☐ 17. **Make the final selection of your Master of Ceremony/ Auctioneer**

_____

_____

☐ 18. **Have Treasurer check on possibility of accepting credit cards for the evening.**

☐ You'll probably have to pay the nominal fee to use PayPal or an iphone app. It may facilitate Bidding among those who prefer to charge their purchases. Credit card acceptance also limits cash transactions and security problems that can create. Investigate Venmo, PayPal or any other payment methods available.

_____

_____

☐ 19. **Have Ticket Chairman send at least 4 Tickets to members for pre-sale.** Pre-selling of Tickets and Auction pre-Auction parties guarantee more people will come. Having already purchased a Ticket and a special Invitation encourages attendance. Require Ticket Sales, where possible. Encourage Ticket Sale participation by offering an exciting Incentive to the member BRINGING the most people.

_____

_____

1 Month Before Auction

☐ **20. Check on liability insurance**

    ☐ Make sure Auction will be covered under your organization's normal liability insurance policy.

    ☐ If no such coverage, we recommend a special "Event" Policy.

_____

_____

☐ **21. Check with your facility on available chairs and tables**
(See sample layout on page 25.)

    ☐ Walk your facility with your chairmen and decide the following: (See sample layout found on page 25.)

       _ Food and beverage serving areas.

       _ Display tables, walls, and floor space.

       _ Master of Ceremony/Auctioneer's area in front of rows of chairs. (Plan for a center aisle.)

       _ Ticket collection (Check-in area) at door.

       _ Payment (Cashier) area - plan for several (at least 4) Cashiers, even for a small Auction.

    ☐ Arrange for additional rental of chairs/tables as needed.

_____

_____

☐ **22. Have your Food Chairman secure a liquor license,**
if this is required in your community. In our area it is the Alcoholic Beverage Control Department of the State. They will tell you what you will need, if beer, wine, or liquor will be served. Facilities may also be able to guide you through the process.

_____

_____

2 – 3 Weeks Before Auction

☐ **23. Have Your Donation Chairman Call a Donation Meeting to Group Donations Together.**

☐ Decide whether you'll have a Silent Auction. We highly recommend you plan for one, in any case, and have a Silent Auction Chairman ready to go. Only about 70 - 80 Packages can be auctioned off at Live Auction, so you'll need a Silent Auction for the left over items.

☐ **24. Have Donation Chairman arrange all Donations and Certificates based upon results of Donation Committee Meeting.**

☐ Certificates and Letters should be placed in Numbered Envelopes corresponding to the numbers planned for in the Auction Booklet. If you have organizational letterhead envelopes, it adds a nice touch.

☐ Place them in numerical order in a shoe box.

☐ Use small labels to number all Silent and Live Auction merchandise to correspond to numbers in the Auction Booklet.

_____

_____

2 Weeks Before Auction

☐ **25. Contact your Master of Ceremony/Auctioneer and go over their functions for Auction Night.**

_____

_____

1 Week Before Auction

☐ **26. Have Auction Booklet Chairman prepare the Auction Booklet.**

    ☐ Be sure ALL Auction information AND disclosures are included.

    ☐ Include acknowledgement of all Donors and members, who worked on Auction Committees.

    ☐ Have Auction Booklet typed, copied, collated, and cover attached. Be prepared to have an addendum sheet for last minute additions and/or corrections. Put Bidder Numbers on back of each booklet.

Notes

_____

_____

_____

_____

_____

_____

_____

_____

_____

_____

_____

_____

_____

_____

_____

Notes

2 Record Keeping & Goal Setting

Careful accounting of all expenses will help to set next year's budget. Volunteers who spend their own money on expenses, which need to be reimbursed, will also appreciate your organized record keeping methods. Prompt payment of these debts will keep everyone happy and help to keep spirits high.

Either your overall Chairman or your Treasurer can be in charge of this activity.

Careful record keeping by all Chairmen will make your next Event just that much easier to duplicate.

Set the goal of a specific "project" for which you are raising funds, (i.e., a new building, a new wing or other expansion, a mission trip, etc.)

Once you have established that a Goods and Services Auction is to be included in your FUNdraising efforts, the guidelines on the next page may be helpful in meeting projected goals in dollar amounts.

Generally, if you collect merchandise totaling TWO TIMES YOUR GOAL IN RETAIL VALUES, you come very close to meeting the amount of your goal. For example: Your goal is $10,000. Secure $20,000 in retail values of merchandise and services donated. We have found that you will come very close to your FUNdraising goal. Of course, results can be affected by many conditions, such as what the merchandise is and what the demand is for it or the area in which you live, and how large your audience is, etc. These are estimated projections only.

Ticket sale amounts are also important, however, the goal on Ticket Sales is to cover the expenses you've incurred and most importantly to GET PEOPLE TO ATTEND. Efforts should be directed toward getting your members to have LOTS OF PEOPLE THERE, rather than trying to raise money through Ticket Sales.

It is imperative for success that you know where you are going and what you are attempting to achieve. Goals can provide something to shoot for, which motivates your Volunteers; with that in mind, the following may help keep things in perspective. Personalize items to the needs of your own organization:

(Estimated amounts needed)

I. Long term goals (5 years, 10 years, etc.)

A. Building fund   _____

B. Program expansion   _____

II. Short term goals (annual or monthly)

A. Salaries   _____

B. New Equipment   _____

C. Just making ends meet   _____

III. Methods to achieve goals   (Income amounts expected)

A. Long term

  1. Major annual fundraiser

    a. Goods and Services Auction   _____

  2. Ongoing efforts

    a. Thrift Store   _____

    b. Go Fund Me.   _____

B. Short term

  1. Monthly ongoing fundraising efforts

    a. Monthly dues   _____

    b. Raff es   _____

    c. Sales of various fundraising merchandise _____

3 Glossary

Before you get started on your Auction adventure, it will be helpful for you to become familiar with some of the Auction terms listed below.

Auction Booklet A catalog of all Auction Packages. Includes recognition of Volunteers and Donors, as well as, rules for the Event.

Bid An offer by an audience member to purchase a Package.

Bidder Item The Item a customer has Bid upon during either the Live or the Silent Auction. A Bidder Item may have several things in it to make one Package or Item.

Bidder Number Number given to each person on the back of their Auction Booklet. This is their identification number during the Auction.

Bid Price The final amount a customer Bids on an Item.

Bidder Purchase Sheet This begins at the entrance at the check-in table. As people enter they will put down their name, address, and phone. They will be assigned a Bidder Number which will be written down as they fill in the above information. These sheets will be taken to the Cashier's Table during the Auction. Cashier #3 will fill out the purchases made by each Bidder Number. (refer to "Cashier's Instructions" on page 69.)

Cashier's Table Table where people pay at end of Auction.

Certificate Envelope All Certificates or Letters of Authorization from Donors are put into these envelopes. Please note that not all Bidder Items will have Certificate Envelopes.

Chairmen Persons who delegate jobs to other Volunteers, but avoid doing the jobs by themselves.

Check-in Table Where people give a Ticket or pay to enter and receive information about the Auction.

Committee	Selected by the Chairmen or through sign-ups. They work in different capacities to make sure everything proceeds smoothly.
Consignment Item	Donated item requiring a Minimum Price to be returned to the Donor upon sale of item.
Donor	Merchants, friends, members who contribute products, services, or money to the Auction. Those Donors in attendance should be specially recognized.
Donation Sheet	Used to record each individual Donation that comes in.
Door Prize	A MAJOR KEY TO SUCCESS. A major Donation used to be given away at the end of the Auction. Encourages the audience to stay for the entire Auction.
Incentive	Something to motivate people to perform and move to them to action.
Item Description Sheet	The form used for each donated item that comes in. These sheets contain ALL pertinent information needed throughout the Auction process.
Live Auction	An Auction featuring a Master of Ceremony/Auctioneer. Members of the audience raise Bidder Numbers to indicate their interest in a Package or Bidder Item.
Package	Several co-ordinated things put together to make into a Bidder Item.
Retail Value	Value of an item as quoted by the Donor.
Sales Receipt	Each Item in the Silent and each Item in the Live Auction will have a separate receipt. Each customer will be given the same number of sales receipts as the number of Items they purchase.
Silent Auction	Can be done several ways, but typically lesser valued Items are displayed separately and the audience places their Bids on sheets in front of each Item.
Themes	Ties everything together and creates more excitement about the upcoming Event. (Ideas for Themes can be found on page 17.)
Volunteer	Your most prized possession. Must be treated as if they were your most valuable EMPLOYEE!!

4 \ Auction Themes

It is important to build your Auction around a Theme, if possible. A Theme seems to tie everything together and creates even more excitement about the upcoming Event. Be creative with your own ideas, but this will get you started:

Holidays - (avoid planning the Auction on the exact date of a holiday)

Superbowl	Martin Luther King Day
Valentine's Day	Lincoln's Birthday
Washington's Birthday	St. Patrick's Day
Easter	Memorial Day/Veteran's Day
Arbor Day	May Day
Halloween	Christmas/Chanukah
New Year's	Mardi Gras

Labor Day (summer is generally not good FUNdraising time, however.)

Nationalities

Hawaiian	Japanese
Mexican	Etc.

Miscellaneous

Kentucky Derby Day	Spring Fling
Masquerade Party	Hollywood Party
Winter Bliss, etc.	Country Western/Sadie Hawkins Day
1950's/60's Party	

Not only can Invitations and Decorations be designed around the particular Theme, but also Donations and dress codes for the Event can be added for even more FUN. As usual, be creative and let your imagination take over.

Child Volunteer Presenting Hat to Successful Bidder
Mission Viejo Kiwanis Club

5 Securing Volunteers

Depending upon the make-up of your organization, you may have a ready-made Volunteer Network or you may have to ask your members individually to help out with specific tasks. If your members are required to help out on your fundraisers, ask them to sign-up where they are most interested in serving. If, as in most organizations, your membership is willing, try to determine their strengths from your knowledge of the individuals involved and/or from any membership applications which might provide that information and ask for help.

Don't be discouraged by refusals. Just contact the next person on your list.

Try to ask many members to do a small task each, rather than having a few doing everything. Don't have Board Members be the only members actively involved in this project. It is important to get new blood involved and perhaps they will serve on next year's Board. Above all, as the Auction Chairman, assign tasks to others. YOUR PRIMARY DUTY IS MANAGEMENT!

Your best tools are the telephone, the computer and your Telephone Chairman. He or she will keep all your members informed about the Auction and your Donation needs. I would suggest that this person recruit his or her own callers to reach the total membership, when necessary. A telephone and/or email system can be extremely effective here.

Splitting up the work makes this not only bearable, but also enjoyable. This really can be FUN!!

Organizing Committee
Sign-Up Sheet and Responsibilities

Auction Chairman _____

Coordinates entire Event. DELEGATES - DOES NOT DO!!! Makes sure that each Chairman and position performs and things go smoothly. Locates the facility, and recruits Auction Night Helpers (Sign-up sheet found in the back of this book.) This person should be a leader - not a doer, an organized person. A business owner, a manager, an organized wife and mother, etc. would do well in this position.

Donation Chairman _____

Sends out Donation Request Letters; keeps a record of all Donations received; and sends out Thank-you Letters. This person may also collect Donations as they come in. A Donation Committee can be formed, but normally your entire membership gets things donated and actually becomes this Committee. This Chairman should be an organizer, a motivator, a detail person. Sales managers, salesmen, outgoing personalities, office managers, or technically savvy people do well here.

Assistant Donation Chairman _____

This position is not absolutely necessary, but is extremely helpful to Donation Chairman. Sends out Thank-you Letters and works with Ticket and Food Chairmen to get those items donated.

Silent Auction Chairman - Also on Donation Committee _____

Will set-up Silent Auction items and coordinate Silent Auction helpers.

Publicity Chairman _____

Will arrange to have Posters and Flyers designed, printed, and distributed locally. If your organization has a Newsletter or Facebook page, your Publicity Chairman should submit monthly articles. This chairman also submits articles to local media and arranges an email and social media campaign. An organized person with good communication skills, perhaps a writer or an administrative assistant would do well in this spot.

Telephone Chairman - Text Campaign Can Also Be Used _____

Will recruit Volunteers to help with contacting the entire membership regarding possible member Donations and letting everyone know, personally, about the upcoming Auction. Could organize a telephone tree. Someone who loves to talk, but doesn't already work on the phone would do well here. They must be organized and be able to organize others.

Auction Booklet Chairman - Could also be a function of the Donation Committee _____

Works with Donation Committee to locate printer and data entry person. Coordinates Auction Booklet construction and getting it to typist and to printer just prior to Auction. An organized, creative person would be great. Could be a data entry person.

Food Chairman _____

Will determine whether the Event will be catered or if members will donate food themselves. Works closely with Auction Chairman. Coordinates Auction Night Servers. Someone who loves to cook and knows how to serve the proper variety of foods is perfect.

Beverage Chairman - This could also be the Food Chairman _____

Will help to find the best price for wine, beer, coffee, punch, and/or soda, if these are not donated outright. Coordinates beverage servers on Auction Night.

Decorations Chairman - Could be Food/Beverage Chairman _____

Keep it simple. A creative person is ideal.

Ticket Chairman _____

Will be responsible for getting Tickets printed and will coordinate Ticket distribution and sales. Works closely with Donation Committee. A sales personality who can motivate others is great. Could be a salesman or sales manager.

Treasurer _____

Usually the actual Treasurer for the group. Will coordinate efforts of Cashiers on Auction Night and arrange for credit card usage.

Auction Night Volunteers
Sign-Up Sheet and Responsibilities

One month before your Auction, you need to secure the following volunteers for actual event.

Check-In/Ticket Collectors _____

Will collect Tickets or money for admission. Will record name, address, phone number, and assigned Bidder Number for each person on Bidder Purchase Sheet.

Cashiers _____

Treasurer should direct these activities. Other Cashiers will each have specific duties during the Auction and then collect customer money after the Auction. Please refer to "Cashier's Instructions" on page 69.

Food Servers _____

Will watch food tables and keep them stocked with food.

Beverage Servers/Bartenders _____

Will work by the hour. Will serve from the bar until Live Auction begins. After Auction begins, servers become waiters and waitresses circulating through the audience.

Silent Auction Helpers _____

Will watch Silent Auction area to prevent theft and will pick up sheets, when Silent Auction is over. Will also distribute Items to successful purchasers with properly stamped receipt.

Live Auction Helpers _____

Will hand Live Auction Items to Master of Ceremony/Auctioneer and/or demonstrate them to audience. Will also watch Live Auction area toward end of Auction to give Items to successful Bidders with properly stamped receipt.

Hats _____

Will give hats to successful Bidders during Live Auction, get receipt from cashiers, give to Bidder and remove the hat.

* Setup _____

* Cleanup _____

* Setup and cleanup should be specifically pre-assigned for a successful Event

6 Facility Preparation

The most important thing about your facility is to secure it early. Waiting until the last minute causes problems with printing of Invitations and Tickets, Publicity, and the basic security of your entire Event!

Most communities have some place to have your Auction. Churches, schools, and community rooms are perhaps the easiest locations to find and the least expensive to use.

Major hotels, new hotels, etc. can provide good locations, as well. You'll probably have restrictions on the use of outside food and beverage, however, and they tend to be expensive.

It's FUN to try to find an unusual place. We've used an airplane hangar, country clubs, estates, beach and tennis clubs, and a Board of Realtors building. The more unusual the location, the better draw for getting your audience to attend (out of curiosity.) You might even consider a LARGE yacht for your Event.

Just remember that you must have open space enough for your audience to see the Master of Ceremony/Auctioneer and there must be display space (could be an adjoining room or hallway.) We once used a vacant storefront next door to the location.

Always go for the classiest or most unusual location that your group can afford.

Facility Preparation

Staging of the Event is critical. Certain props can be used for various effects. Appropriate music (lively and upbeat to encourage energy and enthusiasm for the Auction Event) should be playing in the background ... this will set the mood! Music can be live or on a CD. Some cultural groups doing FUNdraisers will actually have their own performers provide the musical entertainment background.

Amplification and lighting must be arranged for. Be sure everything is working properly prior to the Auction. Rental of this equipment must be arranged for ahead of time, if the facility does not provide it. A stage makes the best presentation for the Master of Ceremony/Auctioneer, who must be elevated in front of the audience. Would you believe ... we used to use a chair to stand on! We don't recommend that, however, for obvious safety reasons.

Make sure that the Master of Ceremony/Auctioneer is aware of how the chairs and center aisle will be set-up. Be sure there is a center aisle between the chairs and that the chairs comfortably face the stage area. (See sample Facility Layout on the next page.)

Facility Set-up (Before and After)- Dana Point Chamber of Commerce

Facility Layout

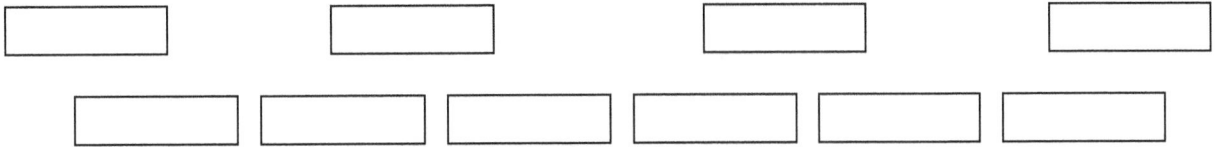

Live Auction Display Area

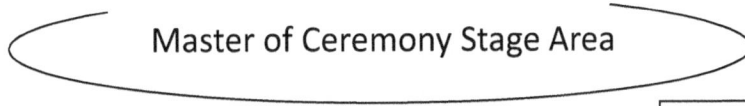

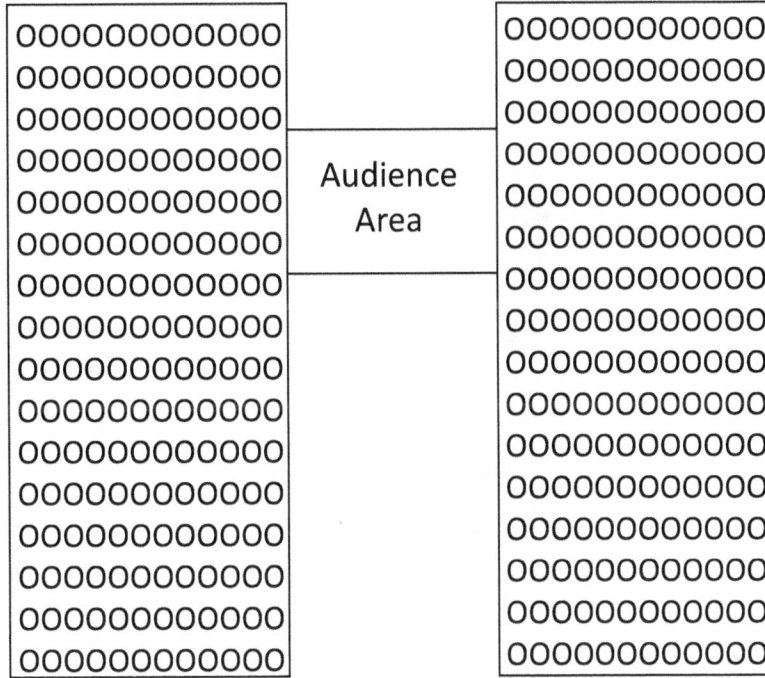

Master of Ceremony Stage Area

CASHIER

OOOOOOOOOOOO	Audience Area	OOOOOOOOOOOO

Silent Auction Tables

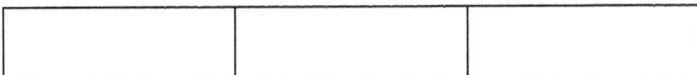

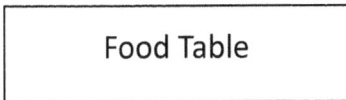

CHECK-IN

BAR

Silent Auction Tables

Food Table

7 Selecting the Master of Ceremony (Auctioneer)

Secret Formula to Selecting Your KEY INGREDIENT

Herein lays, perhaps, the single most important element to the success of your FUNdraising Event. Even if everything else went wrong (which has never occurred at any of our Events) a good Master of Ceremony can "ad lib" to make it a FUN and humorous evening. After all, when you simply have an audience, items donated, and a good Master of Ceremony/Auctioneer, you are virtually assured of making money for your charity or worthy cause.

Always prepare to have a back-up Master of Ceremony/Auctioneer. Perhaps one of the others you've interviewed or a professional Auctioneer in your area could be ready to fill in. We have never missed an Event and the chances of your Master of Ceremony/Auctioneer not showing up that evening are very remote. It is reassuring, however, to know that another Master of Ceremony/Auctioneer is available just in case. Perhaps a team of two people as Master of Ceremony/Auctioneers might work. Plan a meeting with your Master of Ceremony/Auctioneer shortly before your Auction to discuss all the final details.

A Special Message from Cal

Cal Gormick

Master of Ceremony/Auctioneer

The person who will do the best job as a Master of Ceremony/Auctioneer should have the following personality characteristics:

1. You want an "entertainer-type" personality (we all know one or two!). Keep a "Television Game Show Host" personality in mind. Every church, Rotary, Kiwanis, Lions Club, etc. has someone who is very popular and a natural "ham."

    It's amazing how much FUN the Master of Ceremony/Auctioneer can have with the audience. Later we will describe several specific techniques that he/she can use to involve the audience. By the way, when we think of a Game Show Host, we often think of a guy versus a gal. We believe the person's gender is less important than their personality, humor, and popularity on stage.

2. The ideal person would be someone who has been a good Master of Ceremony at other events, i.e., beauty pageants, state fairs, golf tournaments, theatre nights, races, or any similar public event. They would qualify, if they have been a Master of Ceremony at any public or private event.

3. A prominent member of the community, a favorite teacher, or a local radio/TV personality could make a good potential candidate. People whom everyone knows, who are natural "spheres of influence" are excellent.

4. Your Master of Ceremony/Auctioneer must sincerely BELIEVE in the recipient of the funds that will be raised. This commitment makes it a lot easier to press for the funds when, and if, no one Bids for an Item.

5. A person who is a real extrovert, perhaps someone in a sales position would be a good candidate. These people never seem to be at a loss for words!

6. A good Master of Ceremony/Auctioneer will be a good "story teller." He or she will always have entertaining, real-life stories that have happened to them.

Advice for Master of Ceremony/Auctioneer Prior to Event

Your Master of Ceremony/Auctioneer should be interviewed well in advance of your Event and the following points should be discussed:

1. DRESS to the Theme of the Event or, if promotional shirts have been supplied, they should also wear one - perhaps cowboy hats and western shirts, 50's & 60's attire, Roaring 20's, etc. If the Event is a more formal one, a TUXEDO may be in order and is extremely important in establishing the atmosphere of the evening. One such Event we ran was called, "A Night on the California Riviera."

2. Be sure he or she briefly READS the rules and regulations to the audience to familiarize them with the evening's procedures. RECOGNITION OF KEY VOLUNTEERS is very important. The President of your group should fill the Master of Ceremony/Auctioneer in on this information. This is the best source of repayment for your Volunteers' hard work!

   NOTE: Remember that the Master of Ceremony/Auctioneer must have a copy of the entire Auction Booklet at least 2 days prior to the Event so they are completely familiar with each Package. If during the actual Event, he/she doesn't understand what an Item is; that's O.K.! Simply call out to the Donations Chairman, "What's a Who's-Ma-Whach-It?" Ham it up!

3. Take the time to describe each Package and item in it ACCURATELY, being sure to verbally point out ALL LIMITATIONS, RESTRICTIONS, and SPECIAL DEADLINES.

4. Items ON CONSIGNMENT need to be explained to the audience, since there is usually a Minimum Bid where Bidding must begin. Amounts OVER that Minimum will be given to the organization.

5. Donors should be thanked throughout the Event by suggesting that the audience patronize each Donor listed in the Auction Booklet. If Donors who are in attendance that night receive

a special ribbon or other identification at the Event, your Master of Ceremony/Auctioneer should point it out to the audience. This is a great way to let Donors feel like a part of the evening.

6. The audience should be reminded throughout the Auction that the proceeds will be going to whomever is being supported. Many people will spend their money simply by virtue of the giving involved. It is not uncommon for patrons to spend way over the actual full RETAIL VALUE of the Package after being reminded by the Master of Ceremony/Auctioneer why they are there that evening!

7. It is a good idea to let the audience know that you've reached the Retail Value of an Item and that "Bids over that amount go to help the organization and we really appreciate your generosity!" This way your audience knows of your sincerity and will not have buyer's remorse, when they pay double the Retail Value for a Package. They will feel good about spending their money to support the cause.

8. Be sure the Cashiers hear the amounts the Items sold for by Bidder Number and that they hear the final Bid before going on to the next Item. We like to pick out one of our Cashiers and say, "Did you get that O.K., Tim?" If he says, "No," repeat the amount the Item sold for along with the Bidder Number.

9. The audience should never see the Master of Ceremony/Auctioneer's Official Auction Booklet, which has the Retail Values of Packages in it. We have found that people will immediately limit their Bids to approximately half of the Retail Value. If you tell them the Package is worth $500, Bidding will typically slow at $250. The Master of Ceremony/Auctioneer needs to know the values to prompt Bidding as necessary, and answer any questions related to those values.

10. Bidding should be started by the people holding up the back of their Auction Booklet and waving it back and forth. This will help the Master of Ceremony/Auctioneer see their Bid. In case of a tie, the Master of Ceremony/Auctioneer has the right to pick one of them to the best of his or her ability.

Master of Ceremony/Auctioneer's Audience Activities

Since the Master of Ceremony/Auctioneer is part of your entertainment, as well as the one who is selling the Items; the following are some suggestions of FUN activities that will relax the audience and create some exciting things to break the ice or get things moving, if there is a dull moment: (NOTE: Have them choose only 1 or 2, because your Auctioneering time is more valuable.)

Eye-hand Coordination Test: Temple Beth El

1. **Eye-Hand Coordination Test:** Here the Master of Ceremony/Auctioneer should make believe that the President of the United States has asked him/her to conduct an exercise with all of his/her audiences. At first, the audience might think the Master of Ceremony/ Auctioneer is serious! Have the audience put their right hand on their left ear and the other hand on their nose. When the Master of Ceremony/Auctioneer gives a signal, they will switch hands, placing their right hand on their nose and their left hand on their right ear.

   Be sure to practice this a few times, even I get it mixed up at times! Most people have a great deal of difficulty doing this and it looks ridiculous...but do they ever laugh!!! The Master of Ceremony/Auctioneer will then say, "Now, I can see your hands are ready to Bid. You all passed the test!"

2. Before the Event, identify someone who can play an instrument and have them play a song for the audience to guess the title. A great thing for you to do is get a Kazoo (you know, the thing that you hum into and it vibrates the music out.) This lets everyone make music. If you're really talented, get three people on stage and all hum a song together in harmony.

3. If the audience needs to wake-up during the Auction, especially when things are going slowly, a **"Pot Belly Contest"** can be held and becomes a real pick-me-up for audience participation. Remember, however, that if your FUNdraiser is a Black Tie affair, this activity might be too aggressive for the occasion. However, in most cases, it will provide tremendous audience enthusiasm!

Pot Belly Contest: Dana Point Chamber of Commerce

The Master of Ceremony/Auctioneer will call a couple of good looking ladies up on stage and instruct them to pick a few men from the audience who have well-rounded bellies. They come up on the stage for the contest. Participants should be quietly warned that it is for a Pot Belly Contest to avoid possible embarrassment. They should also be free to turn down the request.

The audience is still unaware of what is about to take place! Line up the gentlemen, so the audience can see them. Perhaps you can have them put their arms on each other's shoulder (like a chorus line.) Now tell the audience "these gentlemen have more talent than the rest of us." "We are going to have a Pot Belly Contest and the audience is going to pick the winner." The audience is usually screaming with laughter by now. Have your contestants turn sideways for a profile view!

This is really FUN...we've even had a pregnant woman come up for the contest. She won a special award! The audience picks the winner, by the level of their applause. Have a simple prize ready (meals are excellent as prizes for this one!).

4. Have the audience guess what year the Master of Ceremony/Auctioneer graduated from high school. Someone is sure to say that they graduated much earlier than they really did! The Master of Ceremony/Auctioneer should make sure to "threaten" to charge them "double" for a Bid on an Item later! Perhaps someone who graduated the same year could be brought up on stage for comparison and a comment about who looks better could be made.

5. As corny as this one seems (the Three Stogies made it popular) a "Pie Throwing" Contest still provides an avenue for hysterical laughter and can raise "big bucks," as well!

   Here is a special way to keep the participants clean - A simple 4' x 8' board of either plywood or sturdy cardboard must be made with a hole just big enough to fit your head through. Be sure to bring plenty of towels and put a plastic tarp on the floor. This makes cleaning up easy.

   Pre-arrange a group of participants who are willing to receive a whipped cream pie in the face. The right to throw a pie will be sold to the highest Bidder or Bidders. This will not be announced in the program and will be done at any point in the Auction that the Master of Ceremony/Auctioneer feels things need to be spiced up.

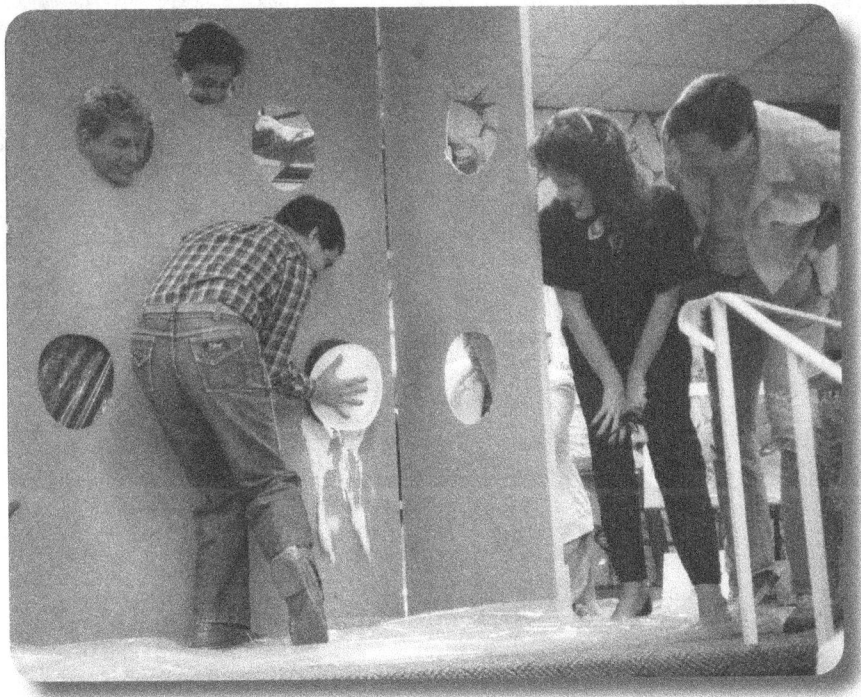

Pie Throwing Contest: Mission Hills Christian School

   At one of our Events the pie throwing episode made $50 per throw and the funniest one was the student who threw a pie in the face of his Sunday School teacher! One of the contestants even paid $50 not to stick his head in the hole!!

6. Hold a "Hairy Leg Contest" in the same manner as the "Pot Belly Contest." Threaten to put hosiery on the one with the "smoothest" legs!

7. Have a special award for the OLDEST person in the audience that night. This should be presented as a moment of sincere respect for a grandparent, etc. based upon the people you observe in your audience that night. Everyone will applaud. You could also have a contest for the youngest adult. Most people will bend the truth here!

8. Hold a "Chubby Bunny" Contest. This is where audience members come up on stage and they will insert marshmallows into their mouth and each time say, "Chubby Bunny." This will continue (without chewing or swallowing) until they can no longer fit marshmallows in and say "Chubby Bunny." Have participants wear an open plastic trash bag around their necks to avoid making a mess.

Chubby Bunny Contest: Mission Viejo Rotary Club

9. Hold an "Animal Sound Calling Contest" in the same manner as the "Pot Belly Contest." Guess the animal! Be ready for a really hilarious Event. People will cry with laughter!

10. Hold an "Impersonation Contest." This could be a celebrity impersonation, an imitation of a prominent local personality, or of a member of your organization. Have the audience applaud for the winner. You won't believe the talent that can be found in your audiences!

11. It is the Master of Ceremony/Auctioneer's job to take the attention off of him/her and to focus it on the audience, just as a good TV Game Show Host would do. There are incredibly talented people in each audience. As you are on stage, concentrate on spotting these individuals for use at a later time in the Event. You know, these are the ones who are always smiling and reacting to the evening's activities! The audience loves to see its members, friends, family, etc. involved in the Event.

Pointers For The Master of Ceremony/Auctioneer During The Event

1. Stories can be related to individuals in the audience, i.e. "You know (referring to a woman in the audience), you remind me of my boss...always giving orders to her husband!"

2. If someone is wearing brilliantly colored clothes, give them some attention! They want it! Their spouses and friends love to see them having FUN. Really "ham" it up!

   Example: "I remember those pants on the golf course at the 15th green last month! They got me so upset that I shot a 12 on the hole!"

3. If you have an autographed football donated, throw it to the biggest guy in the audience several minutes before it comes up for Bid. See if he will let anyone take it away from him in the Bidding!!! Most giants have an equally big ego and will not let anyone take the football away from them. We even had a young lady playfully punch this big guy in the stomach... She really wanted that football!

4. If a Package includes clothing (i.e., jackets, hats, glasses, etc.) pre-arranged models supplied by the Donor can be used. If this is not desired, models can be selected ON THE SPUR OF THE MOMENT from the audience. This is always FUN! Selection should be appropriate to the garment i.e., lingerie should be modeled by an attractive, young woman (just holding it up in front of herself!) Sometimes you can cause hilarious laughter, if a willing man will "model" it! Select an elderly man to model a suit jacket. He will look like a million dollars! Audiences enjoy seeing "real life" people like themselves.

5. "Risqué" Items such as vasectomies, lingerie, etc. should be handled with humorous anecdotes in a clean sort of way. As a general rule, avoid getting these Items donated unless you can handle them! You can ask for help from the audience, while you "play dumb," because you "didn't know any better!" - kind of like the innocent Johnny Carson look!

6. Avoid ethnic, religious, or inappropriate jokes and bad language AT ALL TIMES and under ALL circumstances! Keep this an All American event! Avoid ALL off-color jokes and be careful about politics (unless the Mayor, Congressman, or Senator is there - ham it up with them. They love the free publicity!)

7. Be prepared to recognize and handle certain incompetent Bidders, such as those who've had a bit too much to drink. This rarely happens, but if it does it must be handled delicately, but effectively. Remember, when you recognize a Bidder, they have an obligation to purchase the Item (and pay for it!) If they cannot pay for it...you have lost the sale of that Item to a prior Bidder. Your worthy cause will suffer!

8. Consider having a member of your group on stage with your Master of Ceremony/Auctioneer. This should also be someone with an outgoing personality and someone who is familiar with inside information about your membership. This can make for some real levity. If this person becomes comfortable on stage, they might be able to be the Master of Ceremony/Auctioneer

for subsequent Events. As mentioned earlier, this person will assist the Master of Ceremony/ Auctioneer and can possibly take over in his or her absence, if need be.

9. In a multiple Donation like 5 dental exams from the same Donor, list only 1 in the Auction Booklet. After the Bidding, the Master of Ceremony/Auctioneer will then offer the others for the same price to save time.

10. Be aware of time constraints and keep the Event moving. A mental time picture of which Bidder Item you should be on by what time is helpful. Typically, you start off auctioning Items slower in the beginning of the evening. Don't spend too much time on lesser-valued Packages. You can make three times more money spending time on a larger Package.

11. When you feel tired and discouraged with 30 more Packages left to sell and you're only half way through the Auction, you should psychologically think to yourself that the evening will not last forever. It's only for that night. Just think about auctioning off each Package as quickly as possible. Usually at this point, we speed up the Event substantially and the audience is comfortable with Bidding more quickly. Believe me, you feel just great after the Event, when people come up with the compliments!

12. If the audience appears to be bored or tiring of the current activity, take some time to interject one of the listed activities he/she can do to bring the audience's spirits up, i.e., Pot Belly Contest, Hairy Leg Contest, Impersonations, etc.! This is one of the main purposes for these activities. A peppy, wired up audience will spend more money.

13. A break in the Event is sometimes, but not always necessary. If you have used one of the above-mentioned FUN activities, this is more than sufficient. Remember, if you let the audience leave their seats, it is very difficult to get them all back and ready to go in a timely manner.

14. If the audience gets up and leaves, don't panic...they are not the all-important buyers! In fact, even though people are having a FUN time, some have babysitters or other legitimate reasons to go home. These people, however, ARE NOT usually the ones who are spending the money! There always seems to be a dedicated group that is spending the most money and purchasing the most Items.

15. The primary objective of the Master of Ceremony/Auctioneer should be to get through all the Packages and raise as much money for the organization as possible. Remember that your time is limited. Approximately 1 Package every 3 minutes equals 20/hour or 60 Packages in 3 hours. The most I ever auctioned off in one evening was 116. I barely survived! On the low side, we handled only 35. The best average for an evening, we have found, is between 65 - 80 Packages.

There you go ... when all else fails, just relax and have FUN. The audience likes to know that you're a real down to earth person. If you are not prepared, simply adlib! Good luck!!

Cal Gormick, Master of Ceremony/Auctioneer

8   Securing Donations

Always have a goal of the amount you wish to raise. A conservative formula of what to expect from your Donations once they are put up for Auction is approximately 50% of Retail Value. Trips and unique items typically bring a better percentage of their Retail Value. Larger audiences also make for higher Bids.

Think of items that appeal to a large number of people. Strive for a well-rounded group of items with something for men, women, children, teens, families, singles, etc. Sometimes a preschool gets mostly things for young families and forgets those in the audience who might be interested in other items. Sometimes male dominated groups will neglect items for women and children. Obviously, the more diverse your Donations, the better they will sell and the more audience interest will remain.

Begin within your own organization. Members may own a vacation home, a boat, or a motor home among other items. Members may also know people who have these items.

KEY TO SUCCESS: The real secret to obtaining great Donations is "networking". You might ask yourselves, "Who do you know who has...?"

Members may own businesses they would like to promote through a Donation of a product or service that would demonstrate their business to friends and acquaintances.

Donation Training: Placentia Foundation

Donation Suggestions

Check the Internet for the phone numbers and addresses for possible Donors listed below. Always contact new establishments and suggest the advertising benefits connected with making a Donation within the local community. Be creative and try all avenues, no matter how crazy they sound at the time! You can have literally anything you want or can dream of!

❑ RESTAURANTS

    ❑ It is generally best to contact the local facility, when you are dealing with a chain of stores. Always ask for the name of the owner/manager and speak only to him/her.

    ❑ Hamburger, pizza and ice cream stores can be used in birthday packages. Generally places catering to children are good for this.

❑ RESORTS

    ❑ Weekends and weeks away at members' private condos, cabins and timeshares. (Timeshare note: Perhaps a Donation can be found through a timeshare exchange program. Maybe a British castle, a houseboat, or something in Europe or Asia.)

❑ SPECIALTY ITEMS

    ❑ Professional football team - signed football

    ❑ Signed baseball mitt

    ❑ Sporting goods stores - ski/surf items, items relating to your organization.

    ❑ Religious Items

    ❑ Dinner/lunch with an important member of your organization. Lunch or meeting with local personality (mayor, city council, etc.)

    ❑ Lessons from Little League Coach; bake cookies with a teacher or the principal; tutoring from a favorite teacher; brainstorm with what relates to your organization.

    ❑ Vintage Automobiles - maybe from a famous movie. Also try a yearlong lease from a dealer on a new car or 3-month car leases from several dealers over one year.

    ❑ Vintage wine or champagne*

    ❑ Antiques

    ❑ A local university/high school marching band for a private event

*Note: Cal was the Master of Ceremony/Auctioneer at an Auction consisting entirely of exotic wines to raise funds for Diabetes Research.

❏ Local football team or cheerleaders at an event

❏ Hollywood or Broadway participation - request easy things like mementos, personal items, things used in a movie, etc.; rather than a time consuming lunch, dinner or special appearance from a celebrity. Call Screen Actors Guild in Los Angeles at 1-800-SAG-0767 and ask for your star's agent.

❏ Contact local radio stations' Promotion Director to secure an advertising spot, an interview on a talk show or an opportunity to co-host a show.

❏ Contact local magazines and newspapers for advertising space.

❏ SHOWS

❏ Local Events: singers - opera, philharmonic, barbershop, community and college theaters, movie theaters, etc.

❏ AMUSEMENT ACTIVITIES

❏ Raceways (Auto/Horse/Dog)

❏ Local Amusement Parks like Disney World

❏ Area Specialties (harbor cruises, fishing parties - professional or on a member's boat, tramway rides, skiing, skating, bowling, etc.)

❏ Local hotels or resorts

❏ Special areas of interest, e.g., Las Vegas, Atlantic City, the Pocanos, Hawaii, Canada or a local major city.

❏ Airfares - difficult to secure, unless you have a member connected with a travel agency or airline. You might consider taking several cash Donations toward airfare, hotel, etc., to somewhere special.

❏ GENERAL

❏ Case of champagne (suggest to a Realtor - bottles combined in several Packages and their name will be mentioned several times). Realtors should NOT donate reduced fees - these DO NOT sell well.

❏ A visit to a local farm for city slickers or a visit to the big city for farm folk.

❏ Trash cans (from hardware/lumber store can be filled with whatever - sort of a hardware grab bag).

❏ Popcorn tins could be filled with a $50 or $100 bill for extra fun.

❑ Pet stores - who can resist a little creature? Maybe a member has a kitten or puppy for adoption or a farm animal in rural communities.

❑ Exercise places and health spas often donate memberships.

❑ Paper goods and party supply stores

❑ Gymnastics for kids

❑ Florists

❑ Sports places/country clubs - racquetball, tennis, public golf courses (private, if you have a member contact), miniature golf, equestrian centers, etc.

Consider taking cash Donations from business Donors who do not have something that could successfully be auctioned off. Use these cash Donations to purchase a large item, such as a trip, a big screen television, etc. Be sure the collective donor's names are mentioned as the Donors of the Item.

Members can also offer to perform services, such as cleaning, car washing, baby-sitting, etc. Dinners cooked by "gourmet experts" among your membership sell very well at Auction.

Always start with the sources at your fingertips. Some groups never have to go beyond their own people and their contacts. Your Donation Committee can be helpful in getting the ball rolling by giving their own Donations first.

Your next step would be to divide a list of previous Donors between your Donation Committee. Most of these people will donate again and it will get your Donation Committee off to a good start.

Good Publicity about your organization is extremely helpful prior to FUNdraising and should be encouraged without regard to any other fundraising efforts which may or may not be ongoing. Let the community know who you are and what you do. Work closely with your Publicity Chairman to promote exciting Donations as they come in.

As your Donation Committee approaches local merchants, be prepared. Be sure they know specifically WHY they are asking for the Donation. Have them explain that the FUNdraising Auction is to help cover the cost of new equipment, curriculum, building, etc.

Always try to have Donors underwrite the specific cost of a given item, service or project. Be sure to emphasize the ADVERTISING aspect of donating. Let the Donor know the size of the audience that you expect to be in attendance.

Provide Complimentary Invitations to the Auction for your Donors and a friend. We recommend that Donors receive 2 Complimentary Tickets to your Event. This is a great way to let Donors feel like a part of the evening.

Items on consignment are items that require a certain dollar amount to be returned to the Donor after the item is sold. These items MUST be *bargain priced* for the audience (i.e., a $400 laptop computer with everything over the $400 going to the charity's cause is not a good consignment item!) Had the same laptop been donated at the dealer's cost of, say, $200 for the Minimum Bid, someone obtaining it for $250 would take home a REAL bargain!

NOTE: If possible, avoid ALL Items that require a very high Minimum Bid. It will either cause the Item to be passed or will make very little profit for the organization once the retailer is paid for the merchandise. If not acquired as an outright Donation or with a very low price, your Master of Ceremony/Auctioneer is simply selling the Item for the retailer with little or no benefit to your worthy cause.

Be sure your Volunteers present themselves well. Along with knowledge about your organization, they need to be aware of their mannerisms and the way they are dressed.

Encourage positive mental attitudes! Have them ask for a specific item as a Donation, rather than just anything. This indicates you are not only organized, but that you know something about what the merchant has to offer.

A special technique to get Donations is to get something your Volunteer would like to purchase for themselves. They can come to the Auction and Bid on that Donation, often purchasing it for considerably less than retail. Everyone wins! The organization makes money, the merchant is well received within the community and the Volunteer takes home a bargain!

As items begin to come in, be sure your Volunteers know what has come in already. Donors like to have samples of what others are donating. Merchants, especially, want to be sure they are just as generous as other Donors. They also like to get an idea of what Donations would be appropriate.

Substantial Donations can give your organization added credibility in the eyes of other potential Donors. Constantly network on what you have already - make the most of each Donation!

It is a good idea, wherever possible, to send Volunteers out in pairs to secure Donations. Give Volunteers specific areas to concentrate on, either categories of merchandise or specific geographic territories. (Please refer to the Donation Assignments By Shopping Area found in the back of this book to keep your Volunteers' efforts coordinated.)

Give a person a specific job to do and they will do it. Don't just send them out without this guidance. It's like a child in a toy store. He doesn't know where to begin!

Categories of merchandise can be coordinated into Packages, though generally your first year's effort involves getting whatever you can. In subsequent years, you can fine tune Donations into specific Packages as you begin your Donation solicitation (i.e., a fishing trip on a private yacht, fishing equipment from local sports store, bait from a bait store and food prepared by a local deli).

Donation Committee members should be given weekly deadlines to report back to the Donation Chairman on Donations received or those they are currently working on. This allows the Chairman to attack problem areas without wasting time.

Sample Donation Request Letters, Thank-you Letters, Item Description Sheet can all be found in the back of this book.

Auction Item Description Sheet Instructions

1. Give copies of the Item Description Sheet (Found in the back of this book) to Donation Volunteers along with their Donation Request Letters.

2. Have Volunteers complete ALL information requested as they collect Donations. It is MUCH EASIER to fill in immediately rather than later, when you have to go through papers to locate names and addresses of Donors to prepare the Auction Booklet.

3. Number each sheet consecutively as they come in and insert that Bidder Item Number at the top of each sheet under "Item #."

4. The "Booklet #" is filled in once the Item is placed in a Package and assigned a Bidder Item Number.

5. If your organization meets in a central location, posting copies of the Donations is good for Publicity, and can stimulate ideas for additional Donations. Even if your organization meets in various places, it is possible to post the list on a portable easel or something similar.

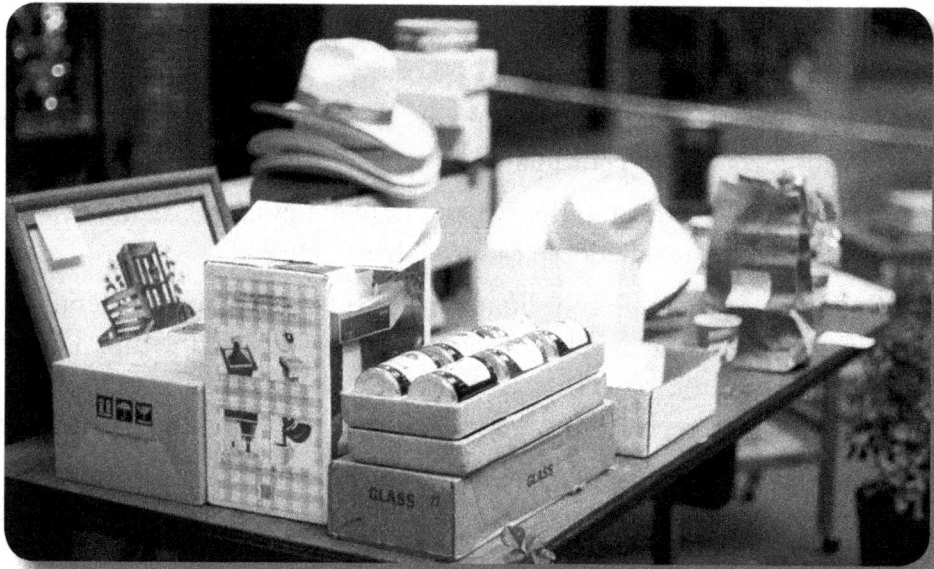

Auction Items to Organize

Donation Committee Meeting

1. Two weeks before your Auction you should hold this meeting. There should be no more than 3 people in attendance. I suggest the Donation Chairman, the Assistant, and either the overall Auction Chairman or perhaps your organization's President. Do not have any more than 3, because you won't be able to come to any prompt decisions.

2. The Donation Chairman should pre-package as much as possible. Use this meeting to get advice on additional items.

3. Everyone should have a list of Donations that have not yet been packaged. Start only after everyone has had a chance to review the list.

4. Make posters showing Donation List and Package Samples (Found in the back of this book.)

5. Start by separating the remaining large or unique items, which will not be combined. Trips will be included on this list, even though they may have luggage or wine, etc. added to them. This will give you a base to start with.

6. Have one person paperclip together Item Description Sheets of items for Packages as they are formed. These will later be numbered and each sheet will have the "Booklet #" filled in accordingly.

7. Separate Item Description Sheets into piles of various categories, such as services, meals, amusements, miscellaneous, etc. Different people can handle each pile to find items as they are needed for a Package.

8. Collectively discuss what would go with what.

9. In a multiple Donation like 5 dental exams from the same Donor, list only one. After the Bidding, the Master of Ceremony/Auctioneer will then offer the others for the same price to save time.

10. As you go, make a separate pile for items, which don't seem to fit anywhere. These can be added as new Packages are created and the ones remaining will become Silent Auction Items.

11. Review the Donation Packages you've created. If time permits, try to secure additional Donations to make these Packages even more complete. (i.e., you have a fishing trip including fishing equipment. Try to get a deli to donate a lunch.)

12. Once all items are combined, decide about the final order for the Auction Booklet. Start with several less valuable Packages, and then space the Items by value saving the best for last. This generates excitement for audience members with smaller Bidding budgets.

13. Be sure types of Packages are also spaced. Don't have too many dinners or entertainment Packages next to one another. Please refer to "Sample Inside Auction Package Listings" found on page 54.

14. Do NOT include Retail Values of Packages in the Booklet, but do include Minimum Bids, if any. The Master of Ceremony/Auctioneer **WILL** have an Official Auction Booklet with Retail Values listed. The audience Bids tend to be higher, if no values are listed. Naturally, gift Certificates can have values listed, (i.e., A $10 certificate from ABC Hair Salon.) Let the Master of Ceremony/Auctioneer announce values verbally and DO NOT let ANYONE see it.

15. Coordinate with your Auction Booklet Chairman to decide upon Auction Booklet Rules and Disclaimers (see sample on page 52) and begin to prepare your Donor Lists. The Donation Chairman will then get all pertinent information to the data entry person.

16. Number your Certificate Envelopes corresponding to the Bidder Item Number assigned for the Auction Booklet as a result of this meeting. Please see the sample below.

> Note: These consecutively Numbered Envelopes will be brought to the Auction in a shoebox and kept securely with the Cashiers. DO NOT DISPLAY any Certificates at either the Silent or Live Auctions. They are too easy to steal.

17. As last minute donations come in, just include them on an addendum sheet, insert them into the Silent Auction, or make them into additional Door Prizes.

18. Begin tagging all things that belong in Packages together. Use labels for small Items and make tags as shown below for larger Items. This will help your Volunteers to set things up for display on Auction Night.

```
YOUR ORGANIZATION
ADDRESS
LOGO (if available)

              Item #_____
              Bidder#_____
```

Envelope Sample

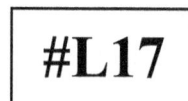

#L17

Self-Stick Label

#L1

Tags

Sample List of Donations (Donation Sheet)

Donation	Donor Item	Bidder Item #	Thank-You Sent/Done
1. Boy's Shorts size 8, child's	Surf City	S1	
2. Child's birthday	McDonald's	L4	
3. Baby blanket	G. Sumpton	L56	
4. Big Bear cabin weekend	Simm's Family	L34	
5. $10 certificate	Mary's Hallmark	L4	
6. 2 Gym lessons	SCATS	S2	
7. 3 Nerfuls toys	Parker Bros.	L56	
8. Bottle wine	ABC Realty	L34	
9. 10 Certificates	Heidi's Frozen Yogurt	L4	
10. 35 Balloons	Creative Balloons	L4	
11. 3-jar Baby Tray	Prince Lionheart	L56	
12. 6-week Lamaze Class	Elaine Newman	L56	
13. Party Cake	Eileen White	L4	
14. $20 in Gas	Mobil Station	L34	

Take the weekend in the cabin first. See what else goes with that. The bottle of wine and the photo transfer to disc make sense. The $20 worth of gas is perfect, since the cabin is within driving distance. The resulting Package, when complete with title would be as follows:

L34) Getting Away From It All

A Weekend at Mr. & Mrs. Simm's Big Bear Cabin. This cabin sleeps 13. Can be used only 5/1/12 -5/3/12. No more than 2 families. ($50 refundable cleaning deposit required;) A bottle of wine from ABC Realty in Irvine; and $20 worth of gas from Jack's Mobil Station in El Toro.

L4) Happy Birthday to You

A Child's Birthday Party (for up to 10 children) at McDonald's in Irvine (after 2:30 P.M.); a $10 Gift Certificates from Mary's Hallmark Store in El Toro; 10 Certificates from Heidi's Frozen Yogurt in Irvine; 35 Balloons from Creative Balloons in Tustin; a Decorated Party Cake from Ann White in Irvine.

Next we saw a baby Package, as follows:

L56) Lullaby...Lullaby

One 6-Week Lamaze Class with Elaine Newman in Irvine, A Baby Blanket made by Gail Sumpton, 3 Nerfuls Toys from Parker Brothers, and a 3 Jar Baby Tray from Prince Lionheart in Irvine.

The remaining items were decided as follows:

The Boy's Shorts were not on a Certificate, so they had limited appeal (i.e., size 8, child) and the Gymnastics lessons didn't seem to fit anywhere, so they both went to the Silent Auction as numbers S1 and S2.

Suggested Package Titles

You can also use song titles, show and movie titles, and familiar phrases to title the Packages. Titling, not only makes your efforts seem more professional; but they also help the Master of Ceremony/ Auctioneer and the audience to locate Packages more easily and allows the Auction to progress more quickly. This can be time consuming, however, and should only be done if you have a willing Volunteer with plenty of time left before going to your printer.

Improving the Image	How Romantic!
Family Fun	Image Making
Christmas is Coming	Getting My Act Together
Mechanics Special	Now You're Cooking
Classy	The Main Event
Taking Care of Mom	Photo Finish
Redecorating	Standing Room Only
Lady's Day	Whale of a Tale
It's a Dog's Life	Rest Period
Cat Nap	Closing Ceremony
Smart Kid!	Day in the Sun
Getting Away From It All	How to Handle a Woman
Gracious Entertaining	M-I-C-K-E-Y---M-O-U-S-E
Company's Coming	Lookin' Good!
Let's Be Patriotic	Eat and Run
Keeping in Shape	Here's Lookin' At You Kid
Collector's Special	Happy Birthday to You...
Special Business	Catch the Mood
That Smile ... That Beautiful Smile	Just Relaxin'
Honeymoon Suite	Check It All Out

Nice House!

Our Last Splurge

Fur Ball

Taking No Chances

Out and About

Crystal Clear

Everything in Place

Cooling Off

Looking Good!

Taking It Easy

Show It Off

Lullaby ... Lullaby

On A Cold Winter's Night...

Getting It Together

Getting Down to Business

Out On the Town

Fixin' Up

Family Time

Time Off

Pot Pourri

Jazz It Up

Firestone

Enjoy

Moving?

Get Me to the Prom on Time

Show Business

Out of Town

Let's Dine Out

9

Auction Booklet Instructions

The cover can be generated by computer as the Mission Viejo Rotary Club did. A sample of the front and back covers may be found on page 51. An artistic member may create a cover as done for the Niguel Parent Participation Preschool or it can be professionally designed and printed as the Dana Point Chamber of Commerce chose to do. The cover design depends entirely upon the resources and finances available to your group.

Important things to remember are that the front and back covers should be made of sturdy paper; that the Bidder Number appears on the back cover of each booklet; and that all of the following are included inside each booklet:

❑ Acknowledgment of Volunteers

❑ General Auction Information

❑ Silent and Live Auction Rules

❑ Listing of All Silent and Live Auction Items

❑ Listing of any Items up for Raffle or used as Door Prizes

❑ And, the all important, List of Donors

Donor ads can be provided to Donors of major items as an Incentive to provide a better Donation. However, the Auction Booklet is not meant to be an ad book. That would just mean more work for your Committee. If you have plenty of Volunteers and a willing individual, it might be something you want to explore. Just be careful not to overdo, especially on your first effort.

Your Auction Booklet should be a full 8 1/2" X 11," so the Master of Ceremony/Auctioneer can clearly see the Bidder Numbers on the back of the booklets.

Development Process for Auction Booklets

1. Line up a data entry person to prepare the Auction Booklet.

2. Coordinate with the Donation Chairman for a final date by which the material can be ready for delivery to the data entry person.

3. Be sure to include a Donor Recognition Page for <u>all</u> Donors, even those just donating pens or pencils for the Silent Auction.

4. Find an artistic member of your group or someone with graphic design expertise to create the cover.

5. Be sure that NO Item values appear in the Auction Booklet except for Gift Certificate values. Printed values can be a psychological hindrance to audience bidding.

6. In a multiple Donation such as 5 dental exams from the same Donor, list only one in the Auction Booklet. After the Bidding on the one, the Master of Ceremony/Auctioneer will then offer the others for the same price to save time.

7. Work with the Donation Chairman to locate a printer with the best rates or another Donor for the printing. Speak with this person (the printer) to determine the lead time necessary to get the Booklet from the data entry person to the printer and back again prior to the Event.

   NOTE: If you are not using a regular printer, you may have to arrange for separate printing of the cover. The cover should be a slightly heavier weight paper for stability. You may also have to get Volunteers to help collate and staple the Booklets to save on expenses.

8. Carefully coordinate the timing between the data entry person and the printer. Don't forget about the possibility of an addendum sheet for late arrivals of Donations.

9. The Booklets must be printed, collated, and stapled. They must also be numbered on the back in consecutive order. This will become the Bidder Number to be held up during the Live Auction.

10. It is IMPERATIVE that the Auction Booklets be at the Auction Facility at least one hour before the doors open to the public.

Auction Booklet Samples

Front Covers can be a simple or professional design and should be 8.5" x 11".

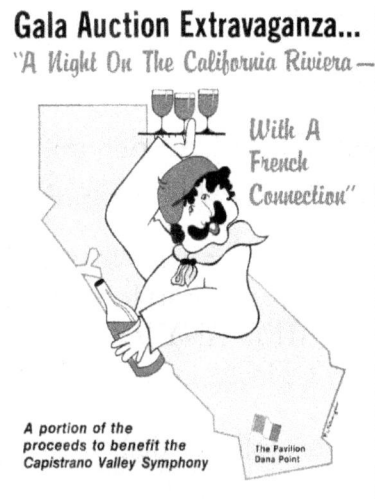

Back cover should be used for bidder number

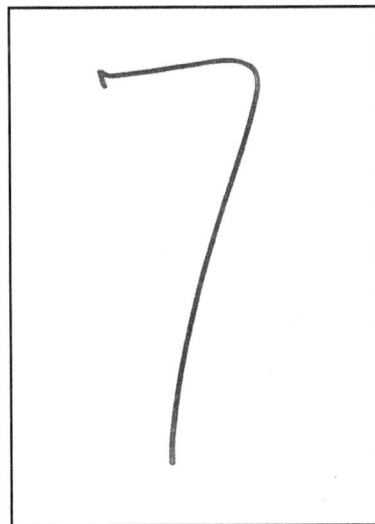

Disclaimers for Auction Booklet

1. Auction items may be removed from display areas only after a STAMPED receipt is issued from the cashier.

2. All Auction items must be paid for and removed from the premises at the close of the evening.

3. Unless otherwise indicated, all items and services must be used before __(1 year after your Auction.)__

4. All sales are final. Auction Items have been donated by friends of __(fill in your organization's name)__ and cannot be exchanged or refunded, except where specified.

5. All items, new or used, are sold "as is" and __(fill in your organization's name)__ makes no representation or warranty with respect to these items or services. __(Your organization)__ DISCLAIMS ANY RESPONSIBILITY OR LIABILITY FOR THE PERFORMANCE OF ANY ITEM OFFERED AT THIS FUNCTION.

6. Payment is to be made by __(fill in cash, credit card or personal check.)__

7. Checks should be made payable to __(fill in your organization's name.)__

8. The Bidder Number for use in the Silent and Live Auctions is found on the back of this booklet.

9. Sales tax shall be applied, as required by law, to some Items (if required in your area.)

Silent Auction Rules

1. Bidder is to write his/her name, Bidder Number on the back of this booklet, and the amount of the Bid on the Bid sheet.

2. New Bids will be written on the first available line on the Bid Sheet.

3. Minimum Bids and Minimum Raises will be indicated on the Bid Sheets.

4. Whole dollar amounts must be used for all Bids. Be prepared to re-Bid on the next available line.

5. Silent Auction will be closed at (set a specific time). The highest Bid at closing time constitutes the winning Bid.

6. The Auction Committee will have final discretion to determine the Winning Bid.

Live Auction Rules

1. Live Auction will begin at   (set a specific time)   and continue without interruption until all of the selected Items have been auctioned.

2. To enter a Bid, raise your Auction Booklet with the Bidder Number on it, directing a signal to the Master of Ceremony/Auctioneer.

3. The highest Bidder acknowledged by the Master of Ceremony/Auctioneer shall be the purchaser. In the event of a dispute, the Master of Ceremony/Auctioneer shall have final discretion.

4. In the event that any opening Bid is not considered by the Master of Ceremony/Auctioneer to be commensurate with the value of the article offered, he or she may reject the same and withdraw the article from the Auction.

Sample Inside Auction Package Listings

Silent Auction

(These may or may not be listed in the Auction Booklet. The Live Auction listings are the critical items to include.)

S 1) Artist's proof by Marilyn Zapp, alumni of the preschool.

S 2) Dinner for Two at The Crown House in Laguna Niguel.

S 3) Family Tickets to Disneyland for up to 6 people.

Live Auction

☐ L 1. FEELIN' GROOVY

Feel groovy with men's and lady's facials from Diane Knox (alumni of Niguel Preschool) then head over to the San Juan Creek Athletic Club. Your Bid on this one will pay for the basic family membership fee. Top it off with the gifts found in Diane's gift basket.

☐ L 2. WHAT THE WORLD NEEDS NOW IS LOVE

This father and child have certainly captured the mood in this print by Marilyn Zapp, alumni of the preschool.

☐ L 3. WHAT NOW MY LOVE?

Actually, that's up to you! We're providing the Palm Desert get-away at the Shadow Mountain Resort and Racquet Club for 2 with two bottles of champagne compliments of Chris Alexander of McCormick Realty, but you'll have to provide the entertainment.

10 Food & Beverage Instructions

Food Table
Niguel Parent Participation Preschool

1. Food can be anything from a sit down dinner to simple hors d'oeuvres, desserts, or just wine and cheese. We recommend that simple food be served, so people can mingle and inspect Auction Items. It becomes a timesaver and won't make the audience feel so full that they are ready to leave before the Auction even begins. A Committee may be needed to get food out and serve it.

   Figure several appetizers per guest and multiply recipes accordingly. Assign several people to each recipe. Be VERY generous on food. It makes a better impression.

2. You'll need to have members indicate the items they plan to bring, unless you have already made specific assignments. It is recommended that specific, simple recipes be provided. Use a sign-up sheet to indicate who is bringing what. This maintains that all-important control.

   (Sample Recipes and Food Sign-up Sheets can both be found in the back of this book.)

3. Members can donate food, they can be reimbursed for their expenses, or the whole thing can be catered - whichever is best for your own group.

   Note: A catered Event can save on time, but can be costly to your final profit. Whatever you can get done by Volunteers will help in the success of your Event.

4. Be sure you have secured necessary paper goods, condiments, silverware, serving utensils, etc. Remember to be as classy as possible. Silver serving items can be borrowed from members and adds a really nice touch.

5. Work closely with your Donation Chairman on Donations of condiments and paper goods (maybe from restaurants or other companies which have their logos imprinted on them.) You should work on finding the best price for wine, beer, coffee, punch, and/or soda, if these are not donated outright. Please refer to "Wine And Beer Quantities" on the next page for quantities needed.

6. Be sure to call the Alcoholic Beverage Control Department in your locality. In our area, this must be done in the last month before the Auction.

Bartender at Dana Point Chamber of Commerce Auction

Wine and Beer Quantities

A 750-ml. bottle of wine holds about 25 oz. of wine. That comes out to five servings of 5 oz. each. Typically, adults will drink about two to three glasses of wine each. For 100 guests, plan on 48 bottles (four cases of wine or the equivalent in wine boxes.) Remember it's important to have plenty of attitude adjustment beverages, so you don't run out. Costco is good because of their return policy, but always be sure to ask.

100 people = 12 bottles of Red Wine, 12 bottles of White Wine, Beer-120 bottles

You might also find The Wedding Alcohol Calculator at TheAlcoholCalculator.com helpful or consult your local liquor outlet for suggested quantities.

Our figures below relate to 100 persons consuming white and red wine and beer. Simply multiply these figures by the number of people you expect at your Event. It is estimated that individuals will consume approximately one drink per hour. Most Auctions will last no more than 3 hours.

50 consuming white wine will total 150 servings of white wine

20 consuming red will total 60 servings of red wine

30 consuming beer will total approximately 90 servings of beer

(Perhaps less since the beers are larger, but some wine drinkers may also have a beer.)

Wine

Each 4 liter bottle of wine serves 33 4 oz. servings. Always round off your results to the next highest bottle.

You'll need the following:

5 4 liter bottles of white wine

2 4-liter bottles of red wine

Figure your prices by simply multiplying the number of bottles you need by the best price you can find.

Beer

Each 1/4 keg serves 100 12 oz. servings. Again multiply the number of kegs you need by the best price you can find. Don't forget to check on deposit costs for the keg and the pump.

Non-Drinkers: Don't forget those who may choose not to drink. In consideration it is recommended that some sort of non-alcoholic punch be available. Sodas are alright, also.

Liquor License: Check with your state's Alcoholic Beverage Control Agency, or the equivalent for restrictions and licenses required in your area.

11   Publicity

1. Secret For Success: Have "hype" from day one! Convince yourselves and others that this is the absolutely best thing coming up!!

2. Use your Monthly Newsletter, Emails or Bulletin. Also consider "trade publications" like religious publications, Club Magazines, blogs and websites.

3. Make large posters to put up in your organization's facility and/or the Auction facility (if it is a different location.) Make posters to show the location of the Auction on the day of the Event. Post these the way you do garage sale signs (i.e., "Auction Here Tonight" with arrows to the facility.) Please be sure this is permitted in your locality and take the signs down after the Auction. Also ask Donors, if you can put your Posters or Flyers up in their shops, blogs, Facebook pages and websites.

4. In addition, distribution of Flyers to Donors, friends of members and around town are great for getting the attendance up. Sometimes grocery stores will put your Flyers into customer's bags for you. Starbucks often has bulletin boards for posting.

5. Invitations and/or emails can also be used as Publicity, when sent to Donors and former members/supporters of the organization.

6. You might consider further Publicity after the Event to announce your success in raising the necessary funds. This will help to keep your organization in the minds of the public. Simply reword your initial Publicity and add a statement indicating that with the additional funds raised you are now able to (insert whatever your initial FUNdraising goals were.) Include a special thanks to the local merchants who made Donations toward the Auction.

7. Keep samples of all Publicity as a reference for following years. Make sure all Publicity is labeled, (i.e., Register 6/18/12.)

Press Releases

Your Publicity Chairman or the one who usually does publicity for your organization can be responsible for this. The first place to go is to look for an online, do-it-yourself event calendar for your target publications. (This is inside information from a friend who is a reporter. She says, "these days newspapers don't have enough staff to create articles, so they direct people to their online calendar." She thinks many other publications have something similar. They also don't run calendars in print. No space. The do-it-yourself event calendar at her paper is great, because you can submit photos and maps, go into great detail and set your own keywords to improve readership. Sometimes people unrelated to your Event are just looking for something to do. They might just happen onto your Event!)

Local newspapers, television, and radio can also receive Press Release emails. Call each one for required submission dates. Be mindful of magazine deadlines, which are often several months prior to your Event.

Go to the websites of local radio stations, newspapers and local television stations to find email or fax numbers. You want to find the email or number for the main newsroom. Getting the media to insert articles about your upcoming Events involves sending them a Press Release or News Release.

A Press Release or News Release is a clearly stated written communication to the media. These days you don't have to be overly concerned about format. Most Releases are now emailed, so the "style" is what fits in the email body.

Use your organization's logo, if you have one.

The issue really is the news value rather than formatting. I've focused on information related directly to a FUNdraising Auction Event to make it easier for you. Just fill in the pertinent information for your own event.

Start with a real grabber of a first line or headline that will make your purpose for the Release clear to the reporter. The snappier the better, but could be as simple as:

"Exciting Goods and Services, FUNdraising Auction Comes to (Insert Your City)"

The body of the release should be written as you would want it to appear in a news story and it should answer the questions who, what, where, when, why and how. Keep it short, because today reporters are overworked and have little time to waste. Don't put in a lot of fluff. Stick with the basics, similar to the examples below.

Who: Include your own name and contact information (phone & email) at the top of the release, so reporters can contact you for more details. Mention your organization's name in the body of the release (See below).

When and Where: Add the date, time, and location of your event:

(**Who**) "(<u>Name of Your Organization</u>) will be holding their First Annual Goods & Services Auction on (**When and Where**) (<u>Date of the Event</u>) at (<u>Location of Event with Full Address, Including Zipcode.</u>)"

What: A simple sentence listing some of the items that will be available

> (**What**) "Some of the exciting items up for bid are a trip to Paris, a Dallas Cowgirl Signed Football, and Tom Seleck's Baseball Cap."

Why: This should be a short description about why you are holding this event

> (**Why**) "Proceeds from this fun-filled event will go to (Insert the Reason Why You Are Raising Funds)*"

> *Write one or two additional sentences that will tug at the heart strings.

How: Tell readers how to attend.

> (**How**) "Tickets are available at the door for $5.00 per person. For further information, please call (Name and Phone Number of the Contact Person for Ticket Sales.)"

If you have them, offering photos and lists may be helpful. For our purposes, that might mean pictures of the biggest and best donations and/or a list of the top ten donations.

12 Ticket Sales

1. Work with the Donation Chairman to have your Tickets and/or Invitations donated. Sometimes banks or savings and loans will donate the cost of printing. Sometimes food establishments will print a Ticket with a food discount attached.

    Other businesses can be approached, but please don't expect a printing company to donate the entire cost.

2. Ticket stubs or a roll of Raffle Tickets (purchased from an office supply or party store) are recommended for selecting the Door Prize Winner(s).

3. Ticket prices should be only enough to cover the evening's expenses. Your profit should come from the Auction itself. Excessive admission prices will turn people away. GET AS MANY PEOPLE THERE AS POSSIBLE!

    Prices can be as low as $5.00 per person and as high as $50, $100, or even $1,000. It all depends upon your community, the audience you want to attract, and factors relating to your individual organization. Obviously, your pre-Auction expenses will be much higher for Events designed to attract the prominent citizens in the community. BE VERY CAUTIOUS IN THIS AREA.

4. Even if every expense is covered through Donations, it is still important to charge SOMETHING for admission. This makes the Auction psychologically important to your audience.

5. Send each member at least 4 Tickets to pre-sell or return to you. Pre-selling of Tickets and pre-Auction parties help guarantee people will come.

    Encourage members to invite people to their homes just before the Auction for drinks and then caravan to the Event. Having already purchased a Ticket and a special Invitation encourages attendance.

    Require Ticket Sales, where possible.

Encourage Ticket Sale participation by offering an exciting Incentive to the member bringing the most people. Please refer to "Incentives" on the next page.

Facebook, Evites, etc. can also be helpful to keep track of RSVPs.

6. Two Complimentary Admission Tickets should be sent to all Donors. Coordinate this with Donation Chairman.

   The only exception to this would be, if admission price is very high because you have the audience to support it. In this case, Donors of items worth over a certain amount will be the only Donors to receive Complimentary Tickets.

7. Get an early list of major Donations to distribute during Ticket Sales. Coordinate this with Donation Chairman.

8. Each member or Ticket Seller should be encouraged to write down people who might purchase a Ticket from them (i.e., friends, neighbors, relatives, people from whom THEY'VE purchased something.) Have them begin contacting these individuals first.

9. ABOVE ALL ... emphasize getting PEOPLE TO ATTEND not just selling Tickets.

Incentives

Members and Donors can be encouraged by Incentives in several areas. Some may be applied to your organization.

❏ COMPLIMENTARY TICKETS

Complimentary Tickets can encourage Donors to make a more substantial Donation. Special recognition of Donors of items over a certain value can also be made. Offer to copy their business card on a special Donor Page in the Auction Booklet.

❏ SECURING DONATIONS

An Incentive might be offered to the member bringing in the most Donations or the most valuable Donation.

❏ TICKET SALES

This works especially well if kids are involved. This system was extremely effective for a middle school Auction. Tickets sold for $2.00 each. For every 10 Tickets a child sold, they received $5.00; for every 15 Tickets, $7.50; for 20, $10.00; for 25, $15.00; etc.

This was a profitable program for the kids and the Auction turn out was definitely enhanced by this Incentive Program. Students were encouraged not to sell Tickets door-to-door, but only to those they knew. (Please see sample on next page.)

❏ ATTENDANCE

Give a special prize to the member who has the most guests in attendance. A column should be added to the "Bidder Purchase Sheet" for this. (Found in the back of this book.)

❏ DOOR PRIZE

A major Donation encourages the audience to stay until the end of the Auction. We recommend that there be a minimum of Raffle Prizes. Otherwise the process of selecting and announcing the winners takes way too long!

AUCTION TICKET ORDERS
GODDARD P. T. A. AUCTION
MARCH 18, 2012
PREVIEW 7:15 P.M. AUCTION 8 P.M.

NAME	ADDRESS	PHONE
1.)		
2.)		
3.)		
4.)		
5.)		
6.)		
7.)		
8.)		
9.)		
10.)		

Please make checks payable to Goddard P.T.A. $2.00 donation admission – adults only please. Cash prizes will be awarded to winning ticket sellers. The P.T.A. suggests students do not sell tickets door-to-door but sell to parents, relatives and friends.

Please return order form to school by February 27, 2012. Tickets will be delivered the following week. Thank you.

Ticket Sales Incentive Sample Goddard Middle School

13 Treasurer's Instructions

1. Check on possibility of using PayPal or an iPhone app. to take credit cards for the evening. Audience buying is typically facilitated by credit card availability.

2. Be sure your Cashiers are familiar with their responsibilities. Please refer to "Cashier's Instructions" on page 69.

3. Purchase receipts from an office supply store for use on Auction Night. Be sure to get receipts in duplicate so your organization and the customer can both keep a copy.

4. Make several additional copies of the "Bidder Purchase Sheet" (Found in the back of this book) to be given to the Check-In people at the front door prior to the Auction.

5. Be sure your Check-In people and, then, your Cashiers have some small bills and coins to make change.

6. Be sure one Cashier is familiar with using PayPal or an iPhone app. to work with credit card purchases. The area where the credit card Cashier is located should be clearly labeled, so this Cashier handles only charge purchases. All CASHIERS NEED CALCULATORS or phone with a calculator!

7. Cashiers must have NO OTHER duties on Auction Night. I recommend that your Treasurer be in charge of the Cashiers.

8. If large amounts of cash purchases are expected, consider having your security personnel accompany you to the bank for a night deposit after the Auction. Your local police department may also be able to help.

9. Check on regulations concerning collection of sales tax within your local area. Be sure to follow the applicable laws.

Cashiers at Mission Viejo High School Band Boosters

14

Cashier's Instructions

Each Cashier will rotate the responsibility of making out a customer's receipt as the Live Auction progresses (i.e., Cashier #1 - item #1; Cashier #2 - item #2; Cashier #3 - item #3, etc.) Cashiers should give receipts to people with the hats to give to the successful Bidders. After the Auction, customers will come to the Cashier's Table to pay for their purchases. Once payment is made, the Cashier will stamp the receipt "paid" and the customer may go pick-up their purchase.

> NOTE: Plan to have someone in the audience keep a neat copy of each Bid and winning Bid Number in an Auction Booklet.. This person should have NO OTHER DUTIES THAT NIGHT! This is simply another double check in case things get busy at the Cashier's Table.

The Cashier area may be divided by Bidder Number for larger groups. Just be sure to label the lines clearly, so your audience knows which line to stand in.

The individual jobs Cashiers will perform during the Auction are listed below:

❑ CASHIER # 1 - will get the Bidder Number and Bid Price on each Item in the Live Auction. This will be recorded directly on a copy of the Auction Booklet next to each Item upon completion of Bidding on that Item. This will become a permanent record for your organization. Be sure your Master of Ceremony/Auctioneer acknowledges that you heard the information before he/she proceeds to the next Item up for Bid.

❑ CASHIER #2 - will get the Bidder Number and Bid Price on each Item in the Live Auction. This will be recorded directly on Certificate Envelopes where applicable. These will be kept in the same order as the Items appear in the Auction Booklet. Keep them in a shoebox at the Cashier's Table for customer pick-up after making payment. Be sure your Donation Chairman gives you the envelopes prior to the Auction.

☐ CASHIER #3 - will record the Item Numbers indicating the Items each Bidder has purchased using the "Bidder Purchase Sheet". This information can be obtained from Cashier #1 (for Live Auction Items) and from Cashier #4 (for Silent Auction Items.)

These sheets should be kept for subsequent years. They will indicate purchasers who should be invited to your next FUNdraiser. If something is not claimed at the end of the evening, these sheets will also help to locate the successful Bidder.

Be sure someone has made several copies of this sheet prior to the Auction and that they are given to the Check-In people.

> NOTE: The Bidder Purchase Sheet will be brought to you from the Check-In people as the Live Auction begins. Silent Auction Items will be added after the Master of Ceremony/Auctioneer announces them and sheets are returned to the Cashier's area. Cashier #4 will also need these sheets for recording.

☐ CASHIER #4 - will get the Bidder Number and Bid Price for each Item in the Silent Auction from the Silent Auction Sheets brought to you by the Silent Auction Chairman. This will be recorded directly in the Auction Booklet next to each Item after the Bidding on that Item, if the Silent Auction Items are listed in the Auction Booklet. Will also make up sales receipts from the Silent Auction Sheets given to you by the Silent Auction Chairman after the Silent Auction is closed. Coordinate this with that Chairman to announce the Silent Auction winners and distribute those receipts.

This Cashier will be the first to take customer payments. Other Cashiers will join in after the Live Auction concludes.

> NOTE: Copies of these Instructions should be given to each Cashier so everyone knows what each other is responsible for. (Found in back of this book)

The Cashier Chairman will fill in as needed and keep things running smoothly.

15 Check-In Instructions

1. Make several additional copies of the Bidder Purchase Sheet (Found in the back of this book) for the front door Check-In people prior to the Auction.

2. Be sure your Check-In people and, then, your Cashiers have some small bills and coins to make change.

3. Check-In people will have Auction Booklets already numbered and in consecutive order, ready to be given to people as they give you their Tickets or they purchase one.

4. Check-In people will assign the Bidder Number on the Auction Booklet at the top of the pile. Try to keep the numbers in consecutive order to the best of your ability. Guests will be asked to sign their name, address, phone number, and Bidder Number on the sheet. These sheets must then be given to the Cashiers for further recording purposes, so please do your best.

5. The Door Prize for the evening will be selected by Bidder Number, Ticket Stub or separate Raffle Ticket. The Check-In people must have guests put their Ticket Stubs (if you've made one available) or Bidder Number on a piece of paper into a hat for the drawing later in the evening.

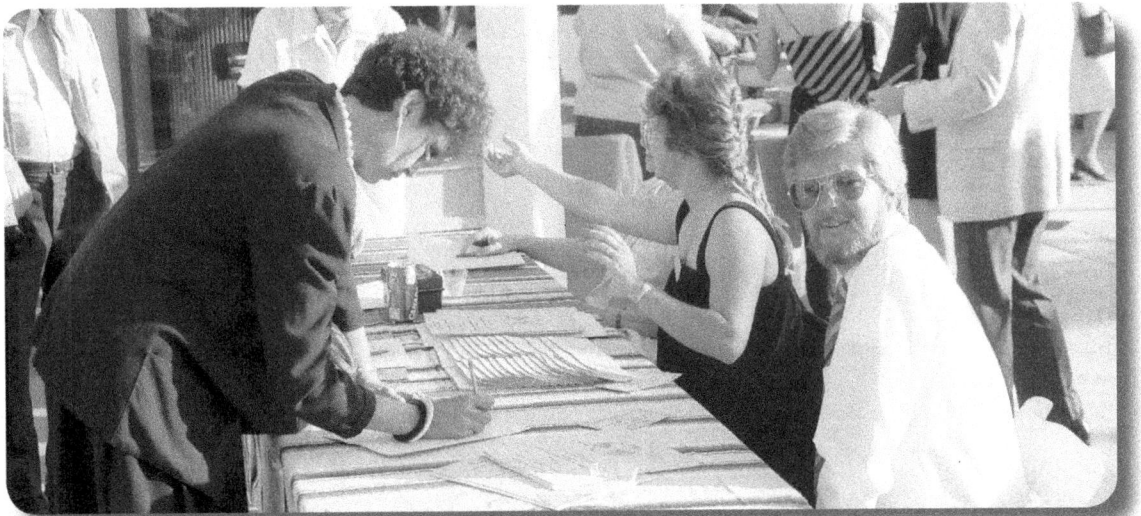

Checking in Customers: Dana Point Chamber of Commerce Event

Silent Auction at I.D.E.A.L. Foundation

16

Silent Auction Information

Plan everything as if you will have a Silent Auction, even if you prefer to have only a Live Auction. It is far easier to cancel plans for a Silent Auction than it is to set up for one at the last minute. Generally, you will get last minute Donations and things that just don't seem to fit into the Live Auction.

1. Plan at least 1 hour prior to the arrival of guests for the Silent Auction set-up, more than 25 Items in the Silent Auction may require more time. Generally setting up the Live Auction Items for display takes less time. Be sure all Items have been labeled or tagged for the number corresponding to the Auction Booklet.

2. Plan for plenty of table space. For each Item in the Silent Auction allow at least one foot of table space (unless the Item obviously needs more). This one foot of space is in addition to the size of the 8 1/2"x 11" Bid Sheet. Have extra tables ready. It is really nice to have them all set up -- just in case. DO NOT place any Certificates on the Silent Auction table (for security reasons these must remain with the Cashiers). Items with Certificates need to be very clear on the Bid Sheets, explaining clearly what is up for Bid.

3. Make placards describing the Silent Auction Items and a Silent Auction Sheet for each Item. These Items must be marked as follows: S1, S2, S3... This avoids confusion with Live Auction Items marked L1, L2, L3...

4. Placing placards describing things with Certificates on a separate Silent Auction table (and numbering them together within the Auction Booklet) facilitates visibility of tangible merchandise.

5. Use Minimum Bids ONLY for the more valuable Items and begin these Minimum Bids at about 40% of Retail Value. You may lower the Minimum Bids during the Silent Auction on Items not getting any Bids ONLY if they do not include things that are on consignment.

6. Remember to bring lots of pens and/or pencils to put on the Silent Auction tables. You might be able to get these from banks or other businesses as a Donation, which will supply them additional advertising. Be sure to include these businesses, as Donors, in the Auction Booklet.

7. Be sure to have several extra Silent Auction Sheets to make corrections and add last minute Items. If you do not have enough Silent Auction Sheets, DO NOT display anything without

them (or an appropriate substitute). This frustrates buyers and can cause them to bother you or your Volunteers about it at a time when you are your busiest. Add them into a Live Auction Package, make them into additional door prizes or save them for the next FUNdraiser.

8. Be sure all display tables are covered with nice paper cloths or lacy ones (these can be borrowed from members). THINK CLASSY at all times.

9. Plan to have someone watching the Silent Auction area at all times. They can answer questions about procedures, keep an eye on things, pick-up sheets as Silent Auction ends and take receipts marked "paid" in exchange for merchandise at the conclusion of the Auction.

10. The Silent Auction will end at staggered times prior to the beginning of the Live Auction. Announcements that SOME of the sheets will be removed should be made periodically before the final conclusion of the Silent Auction. This increases last minute Bidding and excitement in not knowing which will be pulled and which will remain a bit longer.

11. Bidder Numbers of Silent Auction winners should be written on a chalkboard or large poster board, if you have more than 25 Silent Auction Items. This will help in the distribution of the Silent Auction sales receipts. Coordinate this with your Cashiers and let the Master of Ceremony/Auctioneer know when you are ready to have them announced.

12. Give your Silent Auction Sheets to the Cashiers as soon as you have taken down the necessary information on a separate piece of paper. Transfer this information to the above-mentioned board AFTER giving the Silent Auction Sheets to the Cashiers. This will save time in making the final winner announcement.

Typical Auction Agenda

Your guests will enter the facility at a Ticket/Check-in table (mentioned previously.) After paying for or turning in a pre-purchased Ticket, they will provide their contact information and be given a Bidder Number (on the back of the Auction Booklet.) They are then told to refer to the "Bidder Number" on the back of the Auction Booklet and the Auction Instructions in the front of the Booklet. They will then be directed to the Silent and Live Auction display areas, as well as, the food and beverage tables.

Guests can also be pre-registered (possibly using a web-based system like Facebook Events or Evites). List guests alphabetically and assign them a Bidder Number as they enter.

Remember that it is important to obtain the name, address, phone number, and Bidder Number for two reasons. If they fail to claim merchandise, they can be contacted and your organization will also have an invitation list for your next FUNdraiser.

Approximately 1/2 to 1 hour after previewing the merchandise, the Silent Auction is periodically closed and the Live Auction begins. The timing depends on the size of the Silent Auction. About 20 minutes into the Live Auction (when the information has been compiled) a break is made for the announcement of the Silent Auction winning Bids. The Master of Ceremony/Auctioneer announces these in numerical order. The Live Auction then continues without delay. The Live Auction may, however, be interrupted by a drawing for Raffle Items or FUN Activities as needed. If you are planning a Raffle, you'll need Tickets. We also recommend a major Door Prize be reserved for the end of the Auction and be made available only to those present. This will be done by Bidder Number (thrown into a hat by the Check-in people) or with a Ticket Stub, if you've made one available. This will encourage the audience to stay until the conclusion of the Auction.

Upon conclusion of the Auction, people will go to the Cashier area to make their purchases. Both the customer and your organization will receive copies of the sales receipt. A stamped sales receipt will help prevent any possible theft of merchandise.

If all goes well, your customers will go home with some fantastic bargains and your organization will have profited greatly. Your audience will be anxious to attend your next Goods and Services Auction!

Autographed Football: AYSO Soccer

18   Final Details

1. Finalize Publicity Contacts (keeping copies of all Publicity articles, Flyers and Emails for next year.) Make sure Posters are made and put up within the community. Invitations or Flyers should be given to members for their distribution to acquaintances.

2. Call a meeting of all Committees and worker-Volunteers (Food, Beverage, data entry person, Donation, Decorating, Check-in, Cashiers, Silent Auction Helpers, Set-up, Clean-up, and Live Auction Runners.) Be sure they all know how to perform their duties.

3. Make sure you have the necessary liquor license from the Department of Alcoholic Beverage Control (or your area's equivalent,) if alcohol is to be served.

4. Check on PayPal or iPhone app. availability for credit card payments, if you decide to use this method of payment.

5. Be sure to look over your Facility and plan where Food, Beverage, Silent Auction, Check-in area, etc. will be located. This is critical to proper organization. DO IT EARLY!

6. Check on chair and table availability at your Facility. Check over your Silent Auction table requirements.

7. Provide Master of Ceremony/Auctioneer with an Official Auction Booklet or listing of Items at least 2 days prior to Event. Include values on their copy only! Include Minimum Bids, Donors, and special notes, if any. Plan a meeting with the Master of Ceremony/Auctioneer to go over the material.

8. Don't forget to send Thank-you Letters to all Donors (even the late ones!)

9. The night before the Event, carefully double check each item to be sure it has arrived and has been placed in the proper Package. I recommend using little labels to put on all items. They can be easily identified during the Auction and again at the Cashier's Table. It will also help to prevent a Live and Silent Auction Item mix-up. Silent Auction Items should be clearly marked with an "S" next to the Number (i.e., S1, S2, and L1, L2...).

10. Also make neat Envelopes (your organization's logo on them creates a nice touch) with the Package (Item) Number on the outside in bold magic marker or calligraphy. These will be used only for Packages with Certificates or Letters of Authorization.

11. We recommend that a special Item be selected for a Door Prize to encourage people to stay until the Auction is over.

12. DO NOT let ANYONE deliver any Items or Certificates the night of the Auction. This can cause mass confusion.

19 — When It's Over

1. Keep accurate records of Volunteers, Donors, and those who attended the Auction (from Check-In Sheets) for subsequent years. Be sure they are included in the FUNdraising notes passed on to next year's Chairman.

2. Have a final meeting of all Chairmen and provide a written critique of each area based on Chairmen's input. Pass this onto next year's people, also. Include positive, as well as, negative. Make suggestions for areas of improvement.

3. Be sure your Publicity Chairman keeps a copy of all Media Publicity, as well as, copies of Flyers and Posters that were used.

4. Consider adding occupational information to your registration forms or membership applications for new members. This will provide you with ready-made information for potential member Donations.

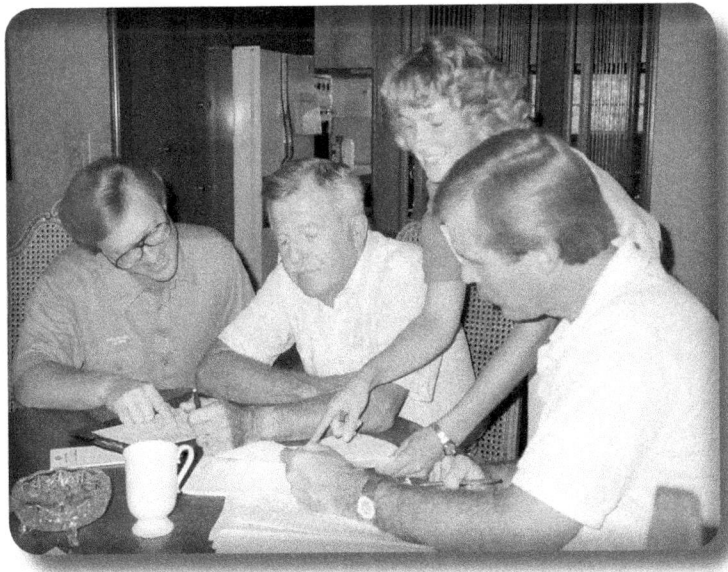

Final Meeting: Laguna Niguel Lions Club

Reproducible Forms, Letters, Checklists, and Recipes

When reproducing forms, the credits listed at the bottom
of each page must remain.

Chairmen Sign-Ups

Securing volunteers for each chair position before starting any activity toward having a FUNdraising Auction is critical! Below you'll find a sign-up sheet for these key Chairmen. In the same manner, begin signing up Auction Night volunteers well in advance. (A sample Auction Night sign-up sheet is also found in this section of Forms.)

Auction Chairman - _____

Donation Chairman - _____

Donation Assistant - _____

Silent Auction - _____

Publicity - _____

Telephone/Email - _____

Auction Booklet - _____

Food - _____

Beverage - _____

Decorations - _____

Tickets - _____

Treasurer - _____

This form was duplicated from the guidebook, *Putting FUN Back Into FUNdraising*, with permission of copyright holder, Cal and Jeanne Gormick.

Donation List for Training Charts

This list should be passed out to your members as your Donation Chairman trains and motivates them on securing Donations.

- ❑ GENERAL
  - ❑ Restaurants
  - ❑ Resorts - Condos, Cabins, Timeshares, Hotels
  - ❑ Specialty Items - Signed football, baseball, mitt
  - ❑ Sporting Goods
  - ❑ Sporting Places
  - ❑ Dinner/Lunch with prominent member of your organization or local community
  - ❑ Lessons/Tutoring - Coach, Teacher
  - ❑ Bake Cookies - with the Teacher or Principal
  - ❑ Vintage Cars
  - ❑ Vintage Wine
  - ❑ Cheerleaders/Football Players
  - ❑ Hollywood/Broadway Mementos
  - ❑ Professional baseball, basketball, soccer, football games.
  - ❑ Museums, government tours, monuments, etc.
  - ❑ Case of Champagne
  - ❑ Trash Can/Grab Bag
  - ❑ Animals
  - ❑ Exercise Places/Spas
  - ❑ Paper/Party Goods
  - ❑ Florists
  - ❑ _____
  - ❑ _____
  - ❑ _____

- ❑ AMUSEMENT ACTIVITIES
  - ❑ Raceways
  - ❑ Local Parks

This form was duplicated from the guidebook, *Putting FUN Back Into FUNdraising*, with permission of copyright holder, Cal and Jeanne Gormick.

- ❑ Area Specialties
- ❑ Museums
- ❑ City tours, government tours, monuments, etc.
- ❑ Professional baseball, basketball, soccer, football game
- ❑ _____
- ❑ _____
- ❑ _____

❑ PERSONAL SERVICES

Your members as well as professionals within the community may also provide these services.

- ❑ Lawn and Garden Services
- ❑ Car Washes
- ❑ Tutoring
- ❑ Baby-sitting
- ❑ Cake Decorating
- ❑ Maid Services
- ❑ Data Processing/Bookkeeping Services
- ❑ Catering Services (several members can get together on this one)
- ❑ Auto/Farm Machinery Repair
- ❑ Limousine Services (member might offer to drive his/her own car)
- ❑ Dinner in the house of a member
- ❑ Attorney Services
- ❑ Accounting Services
- ❑ Lessons (cooking, dancing, tennis, golf, swimming, skiing, sewing, crafts, etc.)
- ❑ Childbirth Instruction
- ❑ Diaper Service
- ❑ Photographs
- ❑ Cosmetic Consultation
- ❑ Color Consultation
- ❑ Interior Design Consultation
- ❑ _____
- ❑ _____
- ❑ _____

This form was duplicated from the guidebook, *Putting FUN Back Into FUNdraising*, with permission of copyright holder, Cal and Jeanne Gormick.

❏ MEDICAL SERVICES

- ❏ Dentistry
- ❏ Podiatry
- ❏ Optometry
- ❏ Orthodontics
- ❏ Chiropractic
- ❏ Surgeon (Vasectomy, Tummy Tuck, Nose Job, Face Lift, etc.)
- ❏ _____
- ❏ _____
- ❏ _____

❏ ANIMAL SERVICES

- ❏ Cat/Dog spay or neutering
- ❏ _____
- ❏ _____
- ❏ _____

❏ BEAUTY

- ❏ Haircuts
- ❏ Perms
- ❏ Coloring/Frosting
- ❏ Manicures
- ❏ Pedicures
- ❏ Acrylic Nails
- ❏ Spa Day
- ❏ Hair Extensions
- ❏ _____
- ❏ _____
- ❏ _____

WHATEVER YOU WANT !!!

Donation Committee Volunteer Assignments

Shopping Center/Area	Volunteer #1	Volunteer #2
1._____	_____	_____
2._____	_____	_____
3._____	_____	_____
4._____	_____	_____
5._____	_____	_____

Categories   Volunteers

1. Hair, nail, make-up services   _____

   _____   _____

2. Doctors, dentists, accountants, attorneys   _____

   _____   _____

3. Home care services (landscaping, housecleaning, etc.) _____

   _____   _____

4. Miscellaneous Services   _____

   _____   _____

5. Restaurants, meals, catering   _____

   _____   _____

Donation Committee Volunteer Assignments (cont'd)

Categories   **Volunteers**

6. Vacations/Sports Activities (health spas, golf, tennis, fishing, etc.)

_____   _____

7. Amusement Areas - (Disneyland, etc.)

_____   _____

8. Lessons (swim, sports, tutoring, etc.)

_____   _____

9. Furniture, antiques, etc.

_____   _____

10. Florists, stationers, gift shops, etc.

_____   _____

11. Business Items (advertising, printing, office equipment)

_____   _____

12. Someone should try to get a local department store to donate nice boxes or bags for the audience to take their purchases home in

_____   _____

Sample Donation Request Letter

Please feel free to reword the following sample Letter for your own organization's purpose. This is meant only as a rough idea of what should be included in a Donation Request Letter. Be sure to use your organization's letterhead for maximum effect. Send potential Donors a copy of this Letter along with the Auction "Item Description Sheet." You may expect to make a personal follow-up to collect the Donations.

(Date)

(Donor)

(Address)

Attn: (Owner/Manager)

Dear_____:

(Your organization) is a nonprofit (type of organization). We specialize in providing (service provided) to (people served). We have proudly served this community for over (amount of time).

So that we may continue to provide these needed services, we hold a major fundraiser each year. This year we will hold a Goods and Services Auction on (date) at (location). By donating a certificate, letter of authorization or actual tangible, personal property, you will not only be helping us to successfully continue our program; but you will be providing yourself with an excellent advertising medium. Your name will be included in the Auction Booklet handed to approximately (# of people) persons expected to attend this event.

You may expect to hear from a member of our Donation Committee in the near future. We also encourage you to join us at the Goods and Services Auction in (month).

Please fill out the Auction Item Description Sheet which is enclosed.

Thank you for your time and consideration.

Cordially,

(your name)

Auction Coordinator

Sample Thank-You Response Letter

Your Donation Assistant, if you have one, can send this Letter. Be sure your letterhead is used. It is suggested that these Thank-you Letters be sent prior to the Auction, as Donations are received. This allows time to send your Donors their Complimentary Admission Tickets. It is also better to send these out prior to the Auction, because you want to be able to relax and just count your profits afterwards. If, however, some of the Letters are sent after the Auction it would be nice to add a statement similar to the following: "with the help of Donors such as yourself, (name of your organization) was able to raise (dollar amount.)"

(Date)

(Donor)

(Address)

Attn: (name of owner/manager)

Dear (name of owner/manager),

The members of (name of organization) wish to express their sincere thanks for your recent donation to our Goods and Services Auction. By donating to this upcoming event, you are enabling us to continue to offer (specific services) to our community.

We truly appreciate your support and look forward to seeing you at our Auction on (date) at (time.) It will be held at (location.) Your complimentary tickets are enclosed.

Thank you, again.

Cordially,

(Name)_____
       Auction Chairman

Date: _____
Items Donated: _____
Recommended Retail Value: _____
Donor: _____
Address - Responsible Party: _____
Restrictions for Use: _____
_____
_____
_____

Auction Item Description Sheet

Item # _____   Booklet # _____

Donated Item: _____

Solicited/Arranged by: _____

How should donor be listed in publicity and the Auction Booklet?

_____

_____

Complete description: (Include interesting facts, model, rarity, type, color, size, expirations, etc.)

_____

_____

Limitations in use: (# of persons, dates, exclusions, geographic limitations, etc.)

_____

_____

How can this item be highlighted? (pictures, brochures, ad work):

_____

Approximate value of donation: _____

Donor's Signature: _____

Address: _____

City: _____ State: _____ Zip: _____

Phone (day) _____ (night) _____

Will item be present at Auction? _____

Will solicitor deliver item? _____ When? _____ By Whom? _____

Will gift certificate be used? _____ Who will prepare? _____

Other comments: _____

Solicitor's Signature: _____

This form was duplicated from the guidebook, *Putting FUN Back Into FUNdraising*, with permission of copyright holder, Cal and Jeanne Gormick.

Bidder Purchases

Bidder #	Name	Address	Phone	Item #'s Purchased	Invited By

This form was duplicated from the guidebook, *Putting FUN Back Into FUNdraising*, with permission of copyright holder, Cal and Jeanne Gormick.

Silent Auction

Minimum Bid: _____   Item #_____

Minimum Raise: _____   Donor_____

Description_____

Bidder Number	Name	Your Bid Amount

Auction Night Helper Sign-Up

Check-in/Ticket Collectors – (up to 4 for large event)

_____   _____

_____   _____

Cashiers   _____   _____

_____   _____

Hats   _____   _____

Beverage Servers:

6:00 – 7:00 - _____   _____

7:00 – 8:00 - _____   _____

8:00 – 9:00 - _____   _____

9:00 - 10:00 - _____   _____

10:00 - 11:00 - _____   _____

Food Servers

_____ _____   _____ _____

_____ _____   _____ _____

Silent Auction Helpers

_____ _____   _____ _____

Live Auction Helpers

_____ _____   _____ _____

Set-up

_____ _____   _____ _____

Clean-Up

_____ _____   _____ _____

Food Preparers

Name	Phone	Item
_____	_____	_____
_____	_____	_____
_____	_____	_____
_____	_____	_____
_____	_____	_____
_____	_____	_____
_____	_____	_____
_____	_____	_____
_____	_____	_____
_____	_____	_____
_____	_____	_____
_____	_____	_____
_____	_____	_____
_____	_____	_____
_____	_____	_____
_____	_____	_____
_____	_____	_____

Recipes for Suggested Appetizers

These recipes are designed to give you an idea of the nice variety of food you can offer at an Event. If it is decided that homemade items will be offered, make copies of these (or other selected recipes) and distribute to your Food Committee. Please note that most of the following recipes require a facility with a kitchen.

Stuffed Mushrooms

Ingredients

2 dozen large mushrooms (remove stems and chop)

6 slices bacon

1/2 green pepper - finely chopped

1/3 onion - finely chopped

2/3 cup bread crumbs

1 tsp. marjoram

1/2 tsp. parsley

Approximately 1 cup chicken bouillon (you want just enough to cover the bottom of the dish. DO NOT cover mushrooms.)

Directions

Fry bacon; remove & crumble. To the bacon grease in the pan, add peppers and onions and chopped mushroom stems. Saute lightly. Remove from pan; combine crumbled bacon, sautéed ingredients and bread crumbs. Bind with 1/2 beaten egg and add seasonings. Stuff caps with the mixture and place in pan containing chicken broth. Be careful not to wet the stuffing mixture. Bake at 350 degrees for 15 - 20 minutes. Makes 2 dozen.

DO NOT ADD BROTH AT HOME, IT WILL BE DONE AT THE FACILITY WHEN COOKED!

Bring a nice tray and parsley sprigs to display mushrooms.

This recipe was duplicated from the guidebook, *Putting FUN Back Into FUNdraising*, with permission of copyright holder, Cal and Jeanne Gormick.

Turnover Dough and Mushroom Mixture

Ingredients

Turnover Dough:

8 oz. pkg. cream cheese, softened

1 ½ cup all purpose flour

½ cup butter or margarine, softened

1 egg, beaten

Mushroom Mixture:

1/2 lb. mushrooms, minced

1 large onion, minced

3 tbles hot butter or margarine

1/4 cup sour cream

1 tsp. salt

1/4 tsp. thyme leaves

Directions

In large bowl with mixer at medium speed, beat cream cheese, 1 1/2 cups flour, and 1/2 cup butter or margarine until smooth; shape into 2 balls; wrap; refrigerate 1 hour. Meanwhile in a 10 inch skillet over medium heat, cook mushrooms and onions in 3 tbles. hot butter or margarine until tender, stirring occasionally. Stir in sour cream, salt, thyme, and 2 tbles. flour; set aside.

On floured surface with floured rolling pin, roll half of dough 1/8 inch thick. With floured 2 3/4 inch round cookie cutter, cut out as many circles as possible. Repeat.

Preheat oven to 450 degrees. Onto 1/2 of each dough circle, place a tsp. of mushroom mixture. Brush edges of circles with some egg; fold dough over filling. With fork, firmly press edges together to seal; prick tops. Place turnovers on ungreased cookie sheet; brush with remaining egg. Bake 12 to 14 minutes until golden. Makes about 3 1/2 dozen.

Do not overstuff! Make these ahead to be reheated at facility. Bring a nice tray and parsley sprigs to display turnovers.

This recipe was duplicated from the guidebook, *Putting FUN Back Into FUNdraising*, with permission of copyright holder, Cal and Jeanne Gormick.

Zucchini Appetizers

Ingredients

3 cups thinly sliced unpared zucchini (about 4 small)

1 cup Bisquick baking mix

1/2 cup finely chopped onion

1/2 cup grated Parmesan cheese

2 tbles. snipped parsley

1/2 tsp. salt

1/2 tsp. seasoned salt

1/2 tsp. marjoram or oregano leaves

Dash of pepper

1 clove garlic, finely chopped

1/2 cup vegetable oil

4 eggs, slightly beaten

Directions

Heat oven to 350 degrees. Grease oblong pan, 13x9x2 inches. Mix all ingredients; spread in pan. Bake until golden brown, about 25 minutes. Cut into pieces, about 2 x 1 inch. Makes about 4 dozen.

Cook at home to be reheated at facility at 350 degrees for 15 minutes.

Bring a nice tray and parsley sprigs to display zucchini.

Artichoke Hearts Wrapped in Bacon

Ingredients

2 cans artichoke hearts (NOT marinated) or 2 pkgs, frozen artichokes (cooked until tender)

Bacon

Directions

Sprinkle with seasoned salt of your choice; wrap in 1/2 slice bacon and secure with toothpick. Broil on both sides.

Cook partially at home. Cooking will be completed at facility.

Bring a nice tray and parsley sprigs to display artichokes.

This recipe was duplicated from the guidebook, *Putting FUN Back Into FUNdraising*, with permission of copyright holder, Cal and Jeanne Gormick.

Sweet-Sour Pork Rolls

Ingredients

3 lbs. lean ground pork
3 cans (5 3/4 ozs. each) water chestnuts,
drained and finely chopped
1 1/2 cups finely chopped green onions (2 to
3 bunches)
1 tbles. finely chopped fresh or crystallized
ginger
2 tsp. salt
3 tbles. soy sauce
4 eggs, lightly beaten
1 1/2 cups packaged bread crumbs
Cornstarch
1/2 cup vegetable oil

(Sweet and Sour Sauce below)

Directions

Combine pork, water chestnuts, green onions, ginger, salt, soy sauce and eggs in large bowl. Mix well with hands; add bread crumbs and mix just until combined.

Chill mixture 1 hour. Shape into 3/4 to 1 inch balls. Roll the balls in cornstarch to coat lightly.

Brown meat balls about 1/4 at a time on all sides in hot oil in large skillet; remove balls to a roasting pan as they brown. Cover loosely with foil.

Bake in moderate oven 350 degrees for 30 minutes or until piping hot.

Makes 36 pork balls.

Sweet-Sour Sauce
makes 6 cups

Ingredients

2 cups unsweetened pineapple juice

1 cup cider vinegar

1/4 cup soy sauce

2/3 cup sugar

1 1/2 cups beef broth

2 tbles. finely chopped fresh or crystallized ginger

1/3 cup cornstarch

2/3 cup cold water

Directions

Combine pineapple juice, vinegar, soy sauce, sugar, beef broth and ginger in large sauce pan. Bring to boiling.

Mix cornstarch with water; add to boiling mixture, stirring constantly. Continue cooking and stirring until sauce is thickened and clear, 1 minute.

Make ahead note: Sauce keeps, covered, in refrigerator up to 1 week. Reheat in heavy saucepan over low heat until bubbly-hot.

Bring in chafing dish. Leave extras at room temperature – then add as needed to hot sauce.

This recipe was duplicated from the guidebook, *Putting FUN Back Into FUNdraising*, with permission of copyright holder, Cal and Jeanne Gormick.

Ham Rollups

Ingredients

1 pkg. ham (8 oz. - wafer thin)

Dash of Worchestershire Sauce

1 container whipped cream cheese with chives

1 3 oz. pkg. cream cheese

Dash on Tabasco Sauce (optional)

Directions

Mix cheese; spread on meat; roll; chill; cut and serve.

Double the recipe...makes about 84 roll-ups.

Prepare at home ready to be served on nice tray with parsley.

Parmesan Chicken Wings

Ingredients

4 lbs. chicken wings – drumstick portion only

1 cup melted margarine

Combine in a sturdy plastic bag:

2 cups grated parmesan cheese

4 tbles. chopped parsley (2 tbles., if using dry)

2 tbles. oregano

4 tsp. paprika

2 tsp. salt

1 tsp. pepper

Directions

Dip in melted margarine and shake a few at a time in bag mixture. Place a single layer in ungreased shallow baking pan. Bake at 350 degrees for 1 hour. Drain on paper towels.

Makes about 50-60.

Do ahead at home and reheat at facility. Bring chafing dish.

This recipe was duplicated from the guidebook, *Putting FUN Back Into FUNdraising*, with permission of copyright holder, Cal and Jeanne Gormick.

Cherry Tomatoes Stuffed with Avocado Egg Salad

Ingredients

2 large ripe avocados

2 tbles. mayonnaise

4 tsp. lemon juice

8 hard-cooked eggs, peeled

Very finely chopped parsley (optional)

1/2 cup finely chopped onion

1 1/2 tsp. salt

1/2 tsp. pepper

About 72 cherry tomatoes, tops removed

Directions

Halve and peel avocado; discard the pit, place the avocado in a small bowl and mash with a fork. Stir in the mayonnaise and lemon juice. Add the eggs, onion, salt, pepper, and parsley. Blend well.

Scoop out cherry tomatoes and turn upside down on paper toweling to drain for several minutes. (A 1/4 tsp. Measure is perfect for scooping out the tomatoes.)

Using a pastry bag with no tip, or a small spoon, fill each tomato. (This can be done up to 8 hours ahead of time.)

Serve on a bed of parsley. Makes 72 tomatoes.

Should be brought on trays with parsley sprigs and ready to be served.

Olive Cheese Puffs

Ingredients

3 cups soft, shredded cheddar cheese

9 tbles. soft butter

1 1/2 cups flour

3 tsp. salt

1 1/2 tsp. paprika

6 doz. olives, stuffed

Directions

Blend cheese with butter; stir in flour, salt, and paprika. Mix well. Wrap 1 tsp. cheese dough around each stuffed olive, completely covering it. Arrange on ungreased cookie sheets.

Bake at 400 degrees until browned, 10 - 15 minutes.

Display on tray with parsley sprigs and bring to facility all prepared. Can be reheated, if desired. Makes 72.

This recipe was duplicated from the guidebook, *Putting FUN Back Into FUNdraising*, with permission of copyright holder, Cal and Jeanne Gormick.

Index

Index

About the Authors

Cal and Jeanne Gormick, a husband and wife team, began their fundraising careers as volunteers for a small Southern California Parent Participation Preschool...

"The year before the school's first Goods and Services Auction, they held an art auction where the audience spent over $10,000. Since the art house brought in the artwork they took about $7,500. The next year the parents decided to solicit their own donations and have Cal act as Auctioneer. That year the audience spent $8,600 providing the preschool with a huge profit! This motivated us to begin training other volunteers to do what we had done and raise money for their organizations through Goods and Services FUNdraising Auctions."

The Gormicks combined Cal's business background in the worlds of venture capital, commercial real estate, and banking with Jeanne's strong background in public relations, marketing and management to provide the elements they needed to train these volunteers.

Cal once served the youth of Southern California as a District Executive for the Boy Scouts of America, which led him to become an emcee at numerous community events and, finally, an Auctioneer for non-profit events.

Jeanne's volunteer activities range from serving as Chairman of their children's school carnival to acting as the Donations Chairman for a local hospital's Golf Tournament.

A FUN fact about this FUN-loving couple is that they were once winners of the "Newlywed Game" emceed by Bob Eubanks.

Cal actually fashioned his Master of Ceremony/Auctioneer role after Bob Eubanks' game show host personality rather than that of a professional auctioneer. In fact, he cautions against using a professional auctioneer. Cal says, "Sometimes a professional auctioneer can make the audience feel pressured or uncomfortable because they lack a true understanding of the grassroots, nonprofit audience."

Like her husband, Jeanne is an accomplished public speaker and trainer.

Together they have trained volunteers to produce successful FUNdraising Auctions from start to finish. They continue to conduct Donation Training Sessions throughout Southern California.

www.ingramcontent.com/pod-product-compliance
Lightning Source LLC
Chambersburg PA
CBHW051224200326
41519CB00025B/7245